CONVENT LIFE OF GEORGE SAND

TO

GEORGE SAND.

A Recognition.

True genius, but true woman! dost deny
Thy woman's nature with a manly scorn,
And break away the gauds and armlets worn
By weaker women in captivity?
Ah, vain denial! that revolted cry
Is sobbed in by a woman's voice forlorn :
Thy woman's hair, my sister, all unshorn,
Floats back dishevelled strength in agony,
Disproving thy man's name; and while before
The world thou burnest in a poet-fire,
We see thy woman-heart beat evermore
Through the large flame.   Beat purer, heart, and higher,
Till God unsex thee on the heavenly shore,
Where unincarnate spirits purely aspire.

ELIZABETH BARRETT BROWNING.

G. SAND

FROM A PAINTING BY COUTURE.

MY CONVENT LIFE

by

GEORGE SAND

From *L'Histoire de Ma Vie*

With a New Chronology of Her Life and Work

Chicago

1978

Cassandra Editions 1977
Chronology © Academy Press Limited 1977

All rights reserved by
Academy Press Limited
360 North Michigan Avenue, Chicago, Illinois 60601

Printed and Bound in the United States of America

Second printing, May 1978

GEORGE SAND: CHRONOLOGY

1804
July 1 Birth at 15 Rue de la Meslay, Paris. Daughter of Maurice Dupin and Sophie Delaborde. Christened Amandine Aurore Lucie Dupin.
Family moves to Rue de la Grange-Batelière, Paris.

1808
Aurore travels to Spain with her mother. They join her father at Palace de Goday in Madrid, where he is serving in Napoleon's army under General Murat.

1809
The family goes to Nohant in France, the home of Maurice Dupin's mother, born Marie-Aurore de Saxe, Comtesse de Horn, the daughter of the illegitimate son of King Frederic-Augustus II of Poland. Death of Maurice Dupin in a fall from a horse.

1810
Sophie Dupin gives custody of Aurore to Madame Dupin in return for a pension.

1810-1814
Winters in Paris at Rue Neuve-des-Mathurins with her grandmother and visits from Sophie. Summers at Nohant.

1817-1820
Educated at the English Convent des Augustines in Paris.

1820
Returns to Nohant. Studies with her father's tutor Deschartres.

1821

Death of Madame Dupin. Aurore inherits some money, a house in Paris and the house at Nohant.
Moves in with her mother at 80 Rue St.-Lazare, Paris.

1822

Meets Casimir Dudevant on a visit to the Duplessis family.
September 10 Marries Dudevant, son of Baron Dudevant. They move to Nohant.

1823

June 30 Maurice is born at Hotel de Florence, 56 Rue Neuve-des-Mathurins, Paris.

1824

Spring and summer at the Duplessis' at Plessis-Picard near Melun; autumn at a Parisian suburb, Ormesson; winter in an apartment at Rue du Faubourg-Saint-Honoré.

1825

Spring at Nohant. Aurore is ill in the summer. Dudevants travel to his family home in Gascony. She meets Aurélian de Sèze, and recovers her health.
November 5 Writes long confession to Casimir about de Sèze. She gives him up.
Winter in Gascony.

1826

Moves to Nohant. Casimir travels, Aurore manages the estate and writes to de Sèze.

1827

Illness again. The water cure at Clermont-Ferraud, where she writes *Voyage En Auvergne,* autobiographical sketch.

1827-1829
Winter at Le Châtre. Summer at Nohant.

1828
September 13 Birth of Solange.

1830
Visit to Bordeaux to Aurélian de Sèze. Their correspondence ceases. She writes a novel *Aimée*.
December Discovery of Casimir's will, filled with antipathy to her.

1831
January 4 Moves to Paris to 31 Rue de Seine.
Joins staff of *Le Figaro*. Writes three short stories: *La Molinara* (in *Figaro*); *La Prima Donna* (in *Revue de Paris*) and *La Fille d'Albano* (in *La Mode*).
April Returns to Nohant for three months. Writes *Indiana*.
July Moves to 25 Quai Saint-Michel, Paris.
December Publishes *Rose Et Blanche* in collaboration with Jules Sandeau. Book is signed Jules Sand.

1832
Travel between Paris and Nohant.
April Solange is brought to Paris.
November Move to 19 Quai Malaquais with Solange.
Indiana and *Valentine* published. Maurice sent by Casimir to Henry IV Military Academy in Paris.

1833
January Break with Sandeau.
June Meets Alfred de Musset.
Publishes *Lelia*.
September Fontainebleau with de Musset.
December 12 To Italy with de Musset.

1834

January 19 The Hotel Danieli in Venice. Musset attempts a break with Aurore, becomes ill. His physician is Pietro Pagello.

March 29 de Musset returns to Paris. Aurore remains with Pagello.

Writes *André, Mattéa, Jacques, Léone Léoni* and the first *Lettres d'Un Voyageur*.

August 15 Return to Paris with Pagello.

August 24 de Musset goes to Baden.

August 29 Aurore to Nohant.

October Return to Paris. Musset return from Baden. Pagello returns to Venice.

November 25 Begins journal to de Musset.

December Return to Nohant.

1835

January Return to Paris.

March 6 Final break with Musset.

Meets Michel of Bourges, her lawyer and political mentor. Writes *Simon*.

Autumn Return to Nohant for Maurice's holiday.

October 19 Casimir threatens her physically. Begins suit for legal separation.

December 1 Judgment in her favor won by default.

1836

February 16 She wins second judgment. Casimir bring suit.

May 10, 11 Another verdict in her favor from civil court of La Châtre. Casimir appeals to a higher court.

July 25, 26 Trial in royal court of Bourges. Jury divided. Out of court settlement. Her fortune is divided with Casimir.

August To Switzerland with Maurice and Solange and Liszt and d'Agoult.

Autumn Hotel de la France, 15 Rue Lafitte, Paris with Liszt and d'Agoult. Meets Chopin.

1837
January Return to Nohant. Publishes *Mauprat* in spring.
Writes *Les Maîtres Mosaïstes*. Liszt and d'Agoult visit
Nohant. Fatal illness of Sophie in Paris. Visit to Fontaine-
bleau, writes *La Dernière Aldini*. Trip to Gascony to recover
Solange, who has been kidnapped by Casimir.

1838
Writes *L'Orco* and *L'Uscoque,* two Venetian novels.
May To Paris. Romance with Chopin.
November Trip to Majorca with children and Chopin.
Writes *Spiridion*.

1839
February Leaves Majorca for three months in Marseilles.
Then to Nohant. Publishes *Un Hiver À Majorque, Pauline*
and *Gabriel-Gabrielle*.
October Occupies adjoining apartments with Chopin until
spring of 1841 at 16 Rue Pigalle, Paris, in winter. Summer is
spent at Nohant with Chopin as guest.

1840
Writes *Compagnon Du Tour De France* and *Horace*. Influenced by Pierre Leroux.

1841
Moves from Rue Pigalle to 5 and 9 Rue St.-Lazare, Square
d'Orléans, with Chopin.

1842
Consuelo published.

1843
La Comtesse De Rudolstadt published, a sequel to *Consuelo*.

1844
Jeanne published, a foreshadowing of pastoral novels.

1845

Tévérino, Péché de M. Antoine and *Le Meunier D'Angibault,* the latter two socialist novels.

1846

La Mare Au Diable published and *Lucrezia Floriani.* Solange married to Auguste-Jean Clésinger. Estrangement from Chopin.

1847

François Le Champi published.

1848

Writes government circulars, contributes to *Bulletins de la Republique* and publishes her own newspaper *La Cause du Peuple,* all for the Second Republic. Death of Solange's son. *La Petite Fadette* published.

1849

Her play based on *François Le Champi* performed at the Odéon. First of a series of successful plays.

1850

Chateau des Désertes published in the *Revue Des Deux Mondes.*

1851

Republic falls. She uses her influence to save her friends from political reprisals. Plays *Claudie* and *Le Mariage De Victorine* presented.

1852

Return to Nohant.

1853

Published *Les Maîtres Sonneurs.* Play *Le Pressoir* presented.

1855

Four volume autobiography *Histoire De Ma Vie* published, carries her life to Revolution of 1848.
January 13 Death of Solange's daughter Jeanne.
Visit to Italy with Maurice and Alexandre Manceau.

1856

Does French adaptation of *As You Like It*.

1858

Holidays at Gargilesse on River Creuse at cottage given her by Alexander Manceau.

1859

Writes *Elle Et Lui*. Publishes *Jean De La Roche* and *L'Homme De Neige*.

1860

Writes *La Ville Noire* and *Marquis De Villemer*.
November Contracts typhoid fever.

1862
May 16 Marriage of Maurice Sand and Caroline Calametta.

1863
July 14 Marc-Antoine Sand born, son of Maurice and Caroline.
Mademoiselle La Quintinie published, anti-clerical novel.
Begins friendship with Flaubert.

1864

Play *Le Marquis De Villemer* presented. Death of Marc-Antoine Sand. Moves from 3 Rue Racine near the Odéon to 97 Rue des Feuillantines. Exchanges Gargilesse for a house at Palaiseau with Manceau.

1865
Death of Manceau.

1866
Visits Flaubert at Croisset, dedicates *Le Dernier Amour* to him. Birth of Aurore Sand.

1867
Return to Nohant to live with Maurice and Caroline. Writes two novels a year.

1868
Birth of Gabrielle Sand.

1870
The play *L'Autre* with Sarah Bernhardt, presented at the Theatre Français.

1870-1871
Franco-German War. Removal to Boussac because of a small-pox epidemic at Nohant.

1876
June 8 Dies.

PREFACE.

THIS little book has been taken from an episode in the published Memoirs of Madame Dudevant, whose maiden name was Aurore Dupin,—that "large-brained woman and large-hearted man, self-called George Sand." The heroine of these pages, the convent schoolgirl, had royal blood in her veins, descended, as she was, from Frederic Augustus, Elector of Saxony, and King of Poland, — her great grandfather, Maurice de Saxe, the famous captain of the war of the Austrian succession, being the illegitimate son of Frederic Augustus and of the once celebrated coquette, Aurore de Königsmark, that unprincipled beauty of whom Charles XII. of Sweden owned himself afraid. But she says in her Memoirs:

" If my father was the great-grandson of Augustus II., King of Poland, and if in this indisputable though illicit fashion I am nearly related to Charles X. and Louis XVIII., it is no less certain that plebeian blood flows in my veins just as directly; and on this side, moreover, there is no bar sinister." In fact her mother, buffeted about in Revolutionary times, was a poor girl, daughter of a Parisian bird-fancier; and from this ancestor George Sand always claimed to have inherited her love of natural history.

The other grandfather was the step-son of the well-known Madame Dupin, the hospitable and enlightened châtelaine of Chenonceaux in its palmiest days. This gentleman, M. Dupin de Francueil, had won for his wife, after a resolute courtship of two or three years, Aurore de Saxe, the widow of Count van Horn, who had been killed in a duel. This lady, educated at Saint-Cyr, and afterward pensioned by the daughter of Marie Antoinette, is the grandmother of "Convent Life." During the Reign of Terror, after the death of her husband, she fell under suspicion, was forcibly separated from her only child, Maurice, then fifteen years old, and imprisoned in the very convent of the Fossés St. Victor, where she afterward sent her little granddaughter to school. The boy was allowed to visit his mother for a few minutes at a time, at long intervals. The buildings were used as a common house of dètention for women; and here, strangely enough, Maurice and Madame Dupin may have encountered the young girl destined later to play such an important part in the lives of both mother and son; for Aurore's mother, Victoire Delaborde, daughter of the old Parisian bird-fancier, had also been arrested on the accusation of singing royalist songs, of which the manuscript was found in her possession, and was imprisoned for weeks in the same place and at the same time with Madame Dupin.

The marriage of her son, while he was

still a young officer in Napoleon's army, was a great disappointment and source of mortification to Madame Dupin, who never became reconciled to the *mésalliance;* and after her father's early death Aurore's childhood was imbittered by the virulent disputes between her mother and grandmother concerning her guardianship and education. She was a bone of contention, over which they were constantly fighting. That these two women should ever agree about anything was so remarkable that no doubt the little girl was reconciled to the idea of the convent school when she found that Madame Dupin's plan of sending her away from home was not opposed by her mother, who accepted it, perhaps, as a compromise; so that after all it is not strange if the life described in these pages seemed like a haven of rest to the loyal daughter and affectionate grandchild.

It is interesting to study the evolution of the idyllic novelist and passionate reformer; to note the characteristic traits of

M. Caro's " mystic pupil of the English convent, the humble adorer of Sister Alicia,
the dreamy, adventurous country-girl," Aurore Dupin, fresh from the moors and
woods of Berri, — and then to recognize
the same peculiarities in George Sand, the
aggressive, uncompromising celebrity of
1831; the apostle of social and domestic
liberty, arraigning the legalized tyranny of
the husband while illogically clinging to
marriage; keenly alive to her own suffering, but ready and eager to relieve that of
others ; open perhaps, even at that late day,
to the charge of sometimes prosecuting the
old " search for the victim," firm believer
as she was in the solidarity of her sex in
the present, past, and future.

After the effervescence of her eccentric
Bohemian career, she led for many years a
quiet, systematic life at her old home, Nohant, indefatigably absorbed in her writing,
her household, and in private theatricals,
and exercising an unfailing hospitality to
literary friends. An unhappy marriage,

followed by a legal separation, had left her with two children, — Maurice and Solange, — whose education the tribunals had confided to her care. Late in life, like Victor Hugo, she took especial delight in her grandchildren, for whom she wrote " Les Contes d'une Grand'mère."

George Sand's earlier works were passionate protests against arbitrary social barriers and separations, — against caste, and the prevailing ideas concerning love and marriage. The idealized sensuality of these novels, however, is redeemed by her subsequent stories, — such idyls as " La Mare au Diable," " François le Champi," and " La Petite Fadette." It has been well remarked that in the " Marquis de Villemer," afterward successfully dramatized, she succeeds admirably in portraying " high life." In fact, the most revolutionary ideas are everywhere clothed by her in expressions of unstudied and habitual elegance. An ardent patriot, her ready pen was always at the service of great ideas, — in 1848, and later in 1871 ; but political compromises were foreign to her nature.

George Sand says of herself : " No doubt I have serious faults; but, like most persons, I am not conscious of them. If we do wrong, it is almost always, no doubt, because we are not aware of it. If we knew better, we should act differently."

Thus the woman of more than seventy years absolved herself in nearly the same words she had used in speaking to her Jesuit confessor so many years before in the English convent of the Rue Fossés de St. Victor.

M. E. M.

CAMBRIDGE, Oct. 1, 1892.

CONVENT LIFE

GEORGE SAND.

———•———

I.

THE English Augustinian Convent Rue
des Fossés St. Victor is one of the
three or four British communities established in Paris in the time of Cromwell;
the only one left unharmed by the French
Revolution. According to tradition, Hen-
rietta of France, daughter of Henry IV.
and wife of the unfortunate Charles I. of
England, often came with her son, James
II., to pray in the convent chapel, where
she touched for the king's evil the crowds
of poor people who flocked about her. All
the nuns were English, Scotch, or Irish, as
well as two thirds at least of the boarders
and lodgers and some of the officiating
priests. At certain hours no French was

allowed to be spoken, not even during recreation, and the nuns hardly ever con-
versed with us except in their native tongue.
They also kept up the national tradition
of taking tea three times a day, and the
favored pupils were sometimes invited to
participate.

The cloisters as well as the church were
paved with long flagstones, covering the
graves of revered English Catholics or notable persons who had died in exile, and who
had been interred by especial favor in this
inviolable sanctuary.   All around, on mural
tablets as well as on the tombstones, were
English epitaphs and verses from Scripture.
In the Superior's apartments, her bedroom
and private parlor, were hung life-size por-
traits of English prelates and princes; and
a conspicuous place was accorded to the
fair and frail Mary Queen of Scots, regarded
as a saint by these pious nuns.

Everything, in fact, was English in the
house, past as well as present; and when
you had once crossed the threshold, it
seemed as if you were on the other side of
the Channel.   For a little country girl like
me the bewilderment of the first impression was overwhelming.

We were received on our arrival by the Superior, Madame Canning, a middle-aged woman, handsome and majestic, whose intellectual sprightliness was in strong contrast with her physical stolidity. Complacent and well-bred, she spoke French with ease, though with a strong English accent, and her expression indicated more resolution and keen sense of humor than any tendency to devout contemplation.

On introducing me, my grandmother showed a little pardonable vanity, saying that I was very far advanced for my age, and that it would be a pity to put me in one of the lower classes. It seemed, however, that there were only two divisions, and the younger one, containing about thirty children, was evidently my proper place. On account of extensive though desultory reading and the consequent development of my mind, they might have created a third class for me, perhaps, with two or three others; but I was entirely unaccustomed to methodical study, and moreover did not know one word of English. I had read with intelligent interest a certain amount of philosophy and a great deal of history; but I was very ignorant, or at all events very uncertain, about the order of events, and while I could have discussed all sorts of topics with more acuteness and discrimination perhaps than some of the teachers, the merest tyro could have puzzled me in regard to facts and their sequence, and I could not have passed a tolerable examination on any subject whatever. I was perfectly conscious of this incapacity, and it was a great relief to hear the Superior say that since I had never been confirmed I must go with the girls of my own age.

It was the hour of recess. Madame Canning sent for one of the pupils, gave me into her keeping with many injunctions, and sent us both to the garden, where I began at once to run about, looking at everything and everybody, and prying into every nook and corner of the playground like a bird making up her mind where she shall build her nest. I was not in the least intimidated, though the other girls looked at me a great deal. I saw at once that their manners were superior to my own, and I watched with interest the older pupils who were not playing, but walked up and down, arm in arm, talking with one another. My guide told me the names of several of these girls, who belonged, it seemed, to very aristocratic families; but that did not impress me at all. I was curious rather to know where all the paths led to, and the names of the chapels and arbors that adorned the garden, and was delighted to learn that I could have a corner plot myself for a garden, cultivating it as I liked. This amusement did not seem very popular; for there was plenty of land from which to choose. But a game of "tag" had been organized; I was put in a "camp," and though I knew nothing of the rules of the game, I did know how to run. When my grandmother came out in the garden with the Superior and the housekeeper, she seemed very much pleased to find that I was already so much at home; but she was about to go, and led me away into the cloisters to say good-by. It was hard for her, and the excellent woman burst into tears when she kissed me. I was really grieved, but thought it right to be brave, and did not shed a tear. Then my grandmother pushed me away and looked at me steadily, exclaiming, "You unfeeling child! you care nothing at all about leaving me, that is very plain;" and she turned away, hiding her face with her hands. I remained standing as if petrified. I thought that I was behaving well, and that since she had brought me there to stay, she ought to be pleased with my courage and resignation. Turning round, I saw near me the house-keeper, Mother Alippe, a kind-hearted little round ball of a woman.

"What is the matter, my dear; what has happened?" she asked in her English accent. "Did you say something that displeased your grandmother?"

"I did not say a word," I answered; "I thought I ought not to."

"Tell me," she went on, taking my hand, "are you sorry to come here?"

Her unaffected kindness unsealed my lips, and I said : "Yes, madam, I cannot help being sorry and lonesome among strangers, where no one loves me; and when I am so far away from my relations, who are very fond of me; but I would not cry before my grandmother, when she has brought me here, and wants me to stay. Was it wrong?"

"No, my child," answered Mother Alippe; "but perhaps your grandmother did not understand. Go and play now. Be a good girl, and everybody will love you here, just as they do at home; only, when you see your grandmother the next time, do not forget to tell her that the reason you did not show any grief at parting was because you did not want to make her feel badly."

I went back to play, but my heart was full. I thought then, and think now, that my grandmother was very unjust. She waited a whole week before she came again, though she had promised to see me in two or three days.

We were cloistered in the strictest sense of the word; for we only went out twice a month, and stayed all night only once a year. There were vacations, but I never had any, my grandmother thinking it best not to interrupt my studies, so as to abridge my stay, and it happened twice that I passed a whole year behind the grating.

We went to mass in our own chapel, and received visits in the parlor, where we also took our private lessons, the professor on one side of the grating and we on the other. All the windows that opened on the street were not only grated, but filled in with white cloth. It certainly was a prison; though with an extensive garden and plenty of companions; but I must say that I was not oppressed by the feeling of captivity, and that the precautions to keep us in, and prevent us from looking out, only amused me. These precautions were certainly reminders of the loss of liberty. The streets into which our windows looked were very dirty and uninviting, and not one of us could have been induced to go out alone at home; but every girl, without exception, took instant advantage of any accident by which the convent door was left ajar and unguarded for a moment, and seized every opportunity to peer through the splits in the white window-shades. To outwit the porter or portress, to run down two or three steps of the flight leading into the yard, to see a hack go by, was the summit of ambition for forty or fifty gay girls, who the next day, perhaps, might walk freely about Paris in company with their parents, without overestimating the privilege, so long as it was not forbidden.

My stay in the convent was marked by three distinct phases, each in turn a source of anxiety to my grandmother, who ought to have known what to expect when she placed me there. The first year I was more

than ever an " enfant terrible," because a
sort of despair, or rather desperation, constantly prompted me to deaden my pain and
drown my homesickness in a sort of intox-
ication. The second year I suddenly became an ardent devotee, and the third was
passed in a state of calm exaltation, of firm
and cheerful piety. The first year I had a
great many scolding letters from my grandmother ; the next she seemed far more
troubled by my devotion than she had ever
been by my mischief ; and the third, she was
pleased, but expressed satisfaction alloyed
by slight uneasiness.

Such in general was the result of my
cloister life; but since a more detailed account may interest those who are curious
in regard to the good and bad influences
of convent education, I shall relate my own
experience in the most unvarnished way,
with perfect sincerity, I trust, of thought
and feeling.

But it may be well to describe first the
convent itself; for the places we inhabit
exert upon our characters an influence almost inseparable from the reminiscences
themselves.

II.

THE English Augustinian Convent was a conglomeration of courts, buildings, and gardens, a sort of village instead of one house; but there was nothing in its aspect to interest an architect or an antiquary. During the two hundred years and more of its existence there had been so many changes, additions, and adaptations, that it was hard to detect the original design. This very heterogeneousness, however, became its principal characteristic. It was mysterious and labyrinthine,—in all its ugliness not devoid of a certain poetic charm with which these recluses knew how to invest the most ordinary objects. It was a whole month before I could find my way about alone, and after all our exploring expeditions I never knew all the winding passages or visited all the recesses of the place. The front on the street was wholly uninteresting; a great, bare, ugly building, with a low, arched doorway that gave access to a wide, steep flight of steps. After mounting these stone stairs (there were seventeen if I remember rightly), you found yourself in a court paved with flagstones and surrounded by low buildings with blank walls, — on one side the church, on the other the cloisters. Adjoining these last was the lodge of a porter, whose duty it was to open and shut the entrance of a vaulted passage communicating with the interior of the convent by a turning-box for parcels, and also opening into four grated parlors where visitors were received, — the first used by the nuns themselves, the second for lessons, and the third, the largest, reserved for the friends and relations of the pupils. In the fourth the Superior received those who asked for her; but she had in another part of the building a still larger grated parlor where she entertained ecclesiastical visitors or members of her own family, as well as those who had any important or confidential communication to make. No other part of the convent was ever seen by men, or even by women, unless they were especially favored; but let us penetrate into the carefully guarded interior.

The door in the court, furnished with a wicket, ground on its hinges as you passed through to the echoing cloisters, — a quadrangular gallery paved with sepulchral stones adorned with death's-heads and crossbones and inscribed with " Requiescat in pace." Through the arches you looked out on the courtyard with its beautiful flower-beds and the traditional well. At one end of the cloisters was the entrance to the church with its adjoining garden, and at the other the new building containing on the ground floor the large schoolroom for the older girls, on the *entresol* the nuns' workroom, on the first and second story the cells of the sisters, and on the third the dormitory for the younger children. The third side of the cloister was that of the kitchens and offices, and led to the cellars as well as to a separate building containing the schoolrooms of the lower classes. Farther on were several other constructions, very ruinous, a perfect maze of dark passages, spiral staircases, little detached buildings, connected with one another by flights of worn and uneven steps, or by boards thrown across. These were probably parts of the original convent, and the attempts to con-

nect them with the whole showed either
lack of means in revolutionary times, or
great stupidity in the builders. There were
galleries that led nowhere, and passages
that you could hardly squeeze through to
strange edifices, that reminded you of those
in bad dreams that shut down upon you
and crush you between the walls that come
slowly together. This part of the convent
baffles description, and the uses to which
these buildings were put were as various
as their grouping. Here lived a boarder,
next door a privileged pupil; farther on was
a room for piano practice, then a linen
storehouse, adjoining vacant apartments occasionally occupied by friends from across
the Channel; with here and there a nook
packed with the miscellaneous objects that
old women, especially nuns, delight in
hoarding, such as dilapidated church or-
naments, strings of onions, broken chairs,
empty bottles, old garments, etc. The
garden was vast, shaded by superb horse-
chestnut-trees. On one side a high wall
separated us from the Scotch convent, and
on the other stood a long row of small
houses tenanted by pious ladies retired
from the world. Besides this garden, there

was also, in front of the new building, a
double quadrangle planted with vegetables,
also bordered by houses, all occupied by
old matrons or by boarding-pupils who had
quarters to themselves. Here was the laun-
dry, and a door that opened on the public
street, only unlocked for the lodgers in the
rows of houses, who had also a parlor for
their own visits. There was yet another
garden, the largest of all, the Garden of
the Hesperides, that we were never allowed
to enter. Here vegetables were cultivated
for the use of the community ; and it was
also full of flowers and fine fruit. We
could see through the high open-work iron
gate bunches of golden grapes, superb
melons, and beautiful variegated carnations ;
but you could only get in at the risk of
breaking your neck. Some of us, however,
ventured to climb over occasionally. Still
beyond was the garden of another sisterhood. I have not mentioned the church, or
the cemetery either, the only parts of the
convent considered remarkable ; but I shall
describe them in the course of my recital.

In this way a hundred and twenty or
thirty nuns, lay sisters, pupils, lodgers, recluses, secular teachers, and servant-maids,

were lodged in the most eccentric manner, often inconveniently, — in one place
crowded together, in another widely scattered over a space where a dozen families
could have lived comfortably, each with a
little land to cultivate. The different rooms
we used were so far apart that fully a quarter
of our time was spent running to and fro.

I have forgotten to speak of the large
laboratory where mint water was distilled, of
the poultry-yard whose emanations poisoned
the air of the children's schoolroom, of the
back room where we breakfasted, of the front
schoolroom, the refectory and the chapter-
house, to say nothing of the cellars and underground passages,— theatres of our future
exploits. But with all this space, the want
of systematic arrangement caused discom-
fort and inconvenience of which it would
be hard to give an idea.

The cells occupied by the nuns were de-
lightfully neat, — tricked out, however, with
knick-knacks devised, framed, colored, and
tied up with ribbons by the patient inge-
nuity of dainty devotees.

In every corner of courts and gardens
grape-vines and jessamine draped the crum-
bling walls. The cocks crowed at midnight

as if they were in the country, and the convent bell rang out with a silvery, feminine tone. In a niche artistically hewn, you saw a pretty conventional madonna of the seventeenth century ; in the workroom rare English engravings represented scenes in the life of Charles I. All, to the wavering light of the little night lamp in the cloisters, and the heavy doors that were swung to and bolted every evening, grating on their hinges, at the end of the reverberating passages, — all was fraught with a mysterious poetic charm to which I became peculiarly sensitive.

My first impressions, however, on entering the children's schoolroom, were very disagreeable ; thirty of us were crowded in a low, small room, with an ugly, glaring yellow wall-paper and a smoky, dilapidated ceiling. The furniture consisted of shabby stools, benches, and tables, with a dirty, smoky stove, and the atmosphere was redolent of bituminous coal and odors from the poultry-yard. The floor was uneven, and a hideous plaster crucifix was the only ornament of the room in which thirty children must pass two thirds of the day in summer and three quarters in winter.

Far more important, however, than surroundings, is giving children into the keeping of persons remarkable for intellect or
character; and I am at a loss to understand
how these nuns, so beautiful and kind themselves, with such distinguished or affable
manners, could have intrusted us to the
care of a woman so repulsive in appearance and bearing as Miss D——, head mistress of the children's division. Corpulent,
untidy, round-shouldered, narrow-minded,
bigoted, and irritable, always harsh and
often cruel, sly and vindictive, ill-tempered
and ill-mannered, — she inspired me at first
sight with the instinctive aversion felt for
her by all my companions. No doubt some
repulsive persons become so conscious of
the effect they produce that they are there-
by incapacitated from helping others, feeling
that they make duty disagreeable merely
by recommending it; and thus they come
at last to care only for their own salvation, irrespective of others, — the most irreligious of all pursuits.

Miss D—— may have been warped in
this way. Not to be unjust, I must say
that she seemed really devout and austere,
— a sort of intolerant, detestable fanatic,

who might have had a certain grandeur
about her if she had lived long ago in the
desert with the anchorites whose faith she
emulated.   In her relations with us her
austerity became ferocious.   It was a joy
for her to punish, a luxury to scold, and
in her mouth scolding degenerated into
abuse.   She was treacherous, too, pretend-
ing to go out (a thing she had no right
to do when she was in charge of the
schoolroom), and listening at the doors so
as to overhear all we said against her
and afterwards entrap us in falsehoods.
Then her punishments were of the most
degrading and humiliating kind.   For instance, she would make us kiss the floor
for what she called "our filthy speech."   It
is true that it was part of the conventional discipline; but the nuns required
only apparent conformity to the regulation,
never seeming to notice that we merely
kissed our hands in stooping to the floor,
while Miss D—— pushed our faces down
in the dust, and would have hurt us if
we had resisted.   It was easy to detect personal resentment in her severity, and she
evidently was constantly enraged because
we hated her.

There was one poor little English girl, five or six years old, a pale, delicate child, named Mary Eyre. At first Miss D—— seemed to try to take an interest in her, with a gleam of something like motherly feeling; but it was so foreign to her brutal, unfeminine nature, that there was an immediate revulsion. When she reproved the poor child she frightened her to death, or excited her to rebellion. Then, not to give way, she would end by shutting her up or even striking her. When at times she tried to joke, or amuse the little thing, it made you think of a bear playing with a grasshopper. Mary often seemed to scream and rebel either from a spirit of revolt or in angry despair; and from morning to night there was a perpetual contest going on, insupportable to witness, between this great coarse creature and the feeble child. But the rest of us did not escape; there was always time left for the ungovernable abuse and condign punishments of which we were all in turn the indignant victims.

I had been content to enter the lower class from an innate modesty not unusual in the children of vain parents; but it was an inexpressible humiliation to find myself in the power of this unsexed tyrant. Her ill-humor was chronic, and I soon incurred her displeasure. Indeed, the first time she looked at me she said, " You seem to be a very idle person," and I was soon ranked with her worst antipathies ; for gayety was repugnant to her, a child's laugh made her grind her teeth, and gladness and youth were criminal in her eyes.

We only breathed freely when a sister came in to take her place ; but that was generally merely for an hour or two in the day. The nuns made a great mistake in coming so little in direct contact with the pupils. We loved them ; for they were all either distinguished, stately, sweet, or imposing. There was a nameless charm about them, and the dress may have had something to do with it; but their presence certainly calmed us as if by enchantment. These cloistered lives, their renunciation of the world and domestic joys, might have been useful to society if they had conse-crated themselves to the work of touching our hearts and forming our minds. The task would not have been a hard one if they had been truly devoted to such a mis-sion ; but they said that they had no time to spare, which was true because of the hours spent in church services and private devotion. That is one objection to convent schools; there are so many secular teachers, female ushers supposed to be pious women, who are unfitted for their work and who tyrannize over the children. Our nuns would have been more meritorious in the sight of God, and it would have been far better for us and our parents, if they had devoted to our well-being — our salvation they would have said — a part of the time they selfishly spent in securing their own.

The nun who occasionally took Miss D——'s place was Mother Alippe, as plump and ruddy as an over-ripe lady-apple that is just beginning to pucker. She was not very gentle, but she was just; and although I did not get along with her very well, we all liked her extremely. Having charge of our religious instruction, one day she asked me where the souls of unbaptized children were languishing. I knew nothing about it, and had never suspected that there could be a place of exile or punishment for these poor little beings, so I boldly answered, " They are in God's bosom."

"What are you thinking of, wretched child!" half screamed Mother Alippe. "Did n't you hear me? I asked you where the souls of unbaptized children dwell."

I was very much confused, and one of the girls, taking pity on my ignorance, prompted me in a whisper, saying, "In limbo," — *aux limbes.* Her English accent deceived me, and sure that she was joking, I repeated, "Olympe," — *in Olympus,* — turning round and bursting into laughter.

"For shame!" exclaimed Mother Alippe. "Are you making fun of the catechism?"

"Excuse me," I answered; "I did not mean to."

My evident sincerity appeased her, and she said, "Since your laughing was involuntary, you need not kiss the floor; but you can make the sign of the cross to recall your thoughts and bring you into a proper frame of mind."

Unfortunately, I did not know how to cross myself. It was the fault of my nurse, who had taught me to touch my right shoulder before the left; and the old priest at home had never noticed the mistake. But when Mother Alippe beheld this enormity, she frowned and said, "Are you doing that on purpose, miss?"

"No, ma'am; what did I do?"

"Make the sign of the cross over again."

"So, Mother Alippe?"

"You have done the same thing again!"

"Certainly, Mother Alippe; what shall I do now?"

"And is this the way you have always made the sign of the cross?"

"Mon Dieu! yes."

"So you swear!"

"Oh, no, Mother Alippe!"

"You miserable child! How have you been brought up? Why, she is a heathen, a real heathen; she says that children's souls go to Olympus. She makes the sign of the cross from right to left, and she says 'Mon Dieu!' when she is not praying. Go and study your catechism with little Mary Eyre; I should not be surprised if she knew more about it than you do."

I was not very much mortified, I acknowledge, and had to try hard to keep from laughing. The convent religion seemed to me so petty and childish that I made up my mind to have very little

do with it, and not treat it seriously.   I
was mistaken; my time was yet to come;
but not till I had left the lower class.   The
atmosphere was not conducive to devotion,
and certainly I should never have been
pious if I had remained under the hated
sway of Miss D—— or the slightly fussy
rule of good Mother Alippe.

III.

ON entering the convent I was not deliberately rebellious, — upon the whole
I was more inclined to docility than revolt;
but when I found myself subject to the
senseless injustice of Miss D——, I enrolled myself resolutely with " les diables,"
for so they called those girls who were not
devout and did not mean to be. The well-
behaved pupils were known as " the good
girls," — " les sages; " and there was an in-
termediate variety that went by the name of
" the stupid ones," — " les bêtes." These
last never took sides with any one, laughing
heartily at the misdemeanors of " les diables," till the teachers or " the good girls "
came in, when they cast their eyes down,
and never failed to say " I did n't do it," as
soon as there was any danger of punishment. The most cowardly among them
even got into the habit of adding, " It was
Mary G—— or Dupin."

I was Dupin, and Mary G—— was the leader of "les diables" in the lower class, the most original girl in the whole convent. She was of Irish extraction, and though only eleven was taller and stronger than I was at thirteen. Her deep voice, her frank, fearless expression and rough, independent manners had obtained for her the nickname of "the boy;" and though she afterwards became a beautiful woman, there was certainly something masculine about her. She was proud and outspoken, remarkable for her strength and agility and still more phenomenal boldness; but her exuberant spirits and constant activity, her heartfelt contempt for anything that was false and mean, excited my unbounded admiration.

On my arrival Mary G—— was away, but was soon described to me as a person above all things to be avoided. In fact, she was the terror of the stupid girls, who naturally tried to enroll me in their ranks. The good girls also were friendly, and put me on my guard against her roughness and petulance, so that I began to be really afraid of what she might do. Some knowing ones told me, in an undertone of conviction, that she was truly a boy, whom her parents were trying to pass off as a girl. She destroyed everything she laid her hands on, she tormented everybody, she was stronger than the gardener, she would not let the girls alone who wanted to study, — in short, she was a plague and a nuisance, and it was useless to try and stop her. " Wait a little," said I to myself. " I am strong, too, and I am not cowardly either. I should like to see any one prevent me from saying and thinking just as I please ! " However, I must say I awaited her return with some anxiety, for I did not like the idea of a hostile element in the class ; it was enough to contend with the common enemy, Miss D——.

Mary came, and I was at once attracted by her open countenance. " Good ! " said I to myself. " I know we shall get along perfectly." But I hung back, since it was for her, an old pupil, to make the first advances. She began by making fun of me : " Dupin, — *du pain*, — some bread ; and then Aurora, the rising sun, — what beautiful names, and what a face, to be sure ! Why, she has a horse's head on a hen's body ! Aurora, I prostrate myself before you, and wish I were a sunflower to salute you the first thing in the morning.   It seems that you call *aux limbes* ' Olympus.'   A pretty education you must have had !   You will be capital fun."

All the girls shouted with laughter, especially the stupid ones, and the good girls did not seem displeased to have one " diable " attack another ; for union is strength. I laughed as heartily as any, and Mary saw at once that I was not thin-skinned.   She went on joking, but in a good-humored way, and half an hour later she gave me a tremendous slap on the shoulder.   It would have knocked down an ox; but I returned it with interest, laughing all the time.

" Say, let us go to walk ! "

" Where ? " I answered.

" Oh, anywhere, so long as it is out of the schoolroom ! "

" How can we ? "

" Don't be a ninny !   Watch me — see what I do, and do the same."

We were all standing, getting up from table.   Mother Alippe was coming along with her books and papers, and profiting by the momentary confusion, but without taking the slightest precaution, Mary walked out unnoticed, and sat down outside in the deserted cloister.   I joined her a few minutes later, but did not say a word. "So here you are," she said. "What excuse did you make to get out?"

"I didn't make any; I walked out just as you did."

"That is the right way. Some girls tell lies, ask permission to go and practise, or pretend that they have bleeding at the nose; others say they want to go and say their prayers in the chapel, — old stories. I won't lie, because it is mean; I go in and out, they ask me questions, and I won't say a word; then they punish me, and I laugh at it. The upshot is that I do as I like."

"I wish I could!"

"Then be a 'diable.'"

"I want to be one."

"Like me?"

"Just like you."

"Well and good," said she, shaking hands. "Let us go back now and behave very well for Mother Alippe; she is an excellent woman. We can save ourselves for Miss D——. Every single evening out of the schoolroom! — do you hear?"

"How do you mean, — out of the school-room?"

"Why, evening recreation in the schoolroom is horribly stupid. We can vanish, coming out of the refectory, and only go back at prayer-time. Sometimes D—— does not notice our absence, and when she does she is enchanted, because she has the pleasure of punishing us when we get back. The punishment is having to wear your night-cap all the next day, even in church. In such cold weather as this it is a capital thing, good for the health, — only when the sisters meet you they make the sign of the cross and say 'Shame;' but that does not hurt anybody. When you have worn your night-cap a great deal for a fortnight, the Superior threatens not to let you go out when your parents send for you; but some-times our relatives coax her, or else she forgets. However, when the night-cap be-comes chronic, she has to keep you in; but I say it is better to lose a day's pleasure once in a while than to have a stupid time all your life."

"I think so too; but what does Miss D—— do when she perfectly hates you?"

"Oh, she abuses you like a fish-wife, — that is just what she is, — and you never say a word, and that enrages her still more."

" Does n't she ever strike you ? "

" She is dying to all the time; but she would have no excuse to give, and she knows that. Some of the good girls and all the stupid ones are afraid of her; the rest despise her and hold their tongues just as we do."

" How many 'diables' are there in the class?"

" Not many, and we need reinforcement, — only Sophia, Isabella, and ourselves. All the others are either good or stupid. Among the good girls there are two — Valentine de Gouy and Louise de la Rochejaquelein — who know as much as I do, only they don't dare to come out. Never mind, though; some of the older girls keep us in countenance, and they will join us to-night."

" What do you do ? "

" You shall see; you are going to be initiated this evening."

You may think with what impatience I waited for night and supper-time. On leaving the refectory recreation began. In summer both classes met in the garden; but in winter the big girls went back to their handsome, spacious quarters, and we were cooped up where Miss D—— forced us to amuse ourselves quietly, — that is to say, not amuse ourselves at all. Coming out of the refectory there was naturally a throng about the door, and I was delighted to see how adroitly "les diables" availed themselves of the confusion they created on purpose to steal away. The cloister was only lighted by one small lamp, which left the other passages almost dark. Instead of walking straight forward to the schoolroom, you slipped aside into the left-hand corridor, let the other girls go by, and you were free.

There I was in the dark with Mary and the other girls she had mentioned. I only remember that evening Sophia and Isabella, who belonged to our class, — two charming girls two or three years older than myself. Isabella, tall, fair, and rosy, was pleasant to look at, but not strictly pretty; very gay and good-tempered and full of fun, especially remarkable for her talent and facility in drawing. She would take a piece of paper, with a bit of charcoal or a spattering-pen, and in the twinkling of an eye you would see hundreds of figures, well grouped, boldly sketched, each one helping to carry out the main idea, that was always

original and often extraordinary. Sometimes there were processions of nuns crossing a gothic cloister, or else a cemetery by
moonlight. The tombs were opening as the
sisters drew near, and the shrouded dead
were beginning to bestir themselves, singing, playing on different instruments, and
inviting the nuns, with extended hands, to
be their partners in a dance. Some of the
sisters were frightened and were running
away and screaming, while the bolder nuns
danced along, dropping veils and mantles
as they whirled and capered with the spec-
tres in the dim distance ; or again, there
were fancy nuns, with goats' feet, or in
Louis XIII. boots, decked with enormous
spurs, displayed as they held up their flow-
ing garments. Her vivid imagination created a hundred ways of representing this
dance of death, for I do not believe that
she knew about it historically. Then there
were sketches of interiors, caricatures of
sisters, pupils, servants, teachers, professors,
visitors, and priests. She was the faithful
chronicler of all the adventures, hoaxes,
panics, and skirmishes, of all the annoy-
ances and all the pleasures of our convent
life. The incessant contest of poor little

Mary Eyre with her tormentor furnished her every day with twenty sketches, each one more pitiful and realistic than the last, and her invention seemed as inexhaustible as our admiration.   Drawing these figures on the sly, at all hours, during lessons, even in the face and eyes of our Argus, sometimes she narrowly escaped detection by rolling up the paper and tossing it adroitly in the fire or out of the window.   That schoolroom stove has thus devoured countless unknown masterpieces.   My retrospective imagination may exaggerate the merit of her productions; but it seems to me that they must have been very remarkable, and would have excited the surprise and interest of a good teacher.

Sophia — Isabella's inseparable friend — was one of the prettiest and most graceful girls in the school.   Her willowy figure was insular in its languid poses; but she had none of the national awkwardness.   Her neck was swan-like, and her small head, beautifully poised, was graceful in every motion.   She had fine eyes; a low, stubborn forehead, shaded by a profusion of shining brown hair; a rosy mouth, pearly teeth, and a blooming complexion (very white for a brunette); and even her ugly nose could not spoil her beautiful face. We all called her " the jewel." Amiable and sentimental, exclusive and enthusiastic in her friendships and implacable in her aversions, she showed dislike by an invincible disdain. Adored by almost all the girls, she only deigned to return the affection of a chosen few. I was devoted to her and Isabella ; but they were rather condescending in their manners : perhaps that was natural, for I was a mere child in comparison.

That night when we first met in the cloister, I saw that all were armed with shovel, tongs, or sticks of wood. Not liking to be the only one without anything in my hand, I ventured back to the schoolroom, seized a large poker, and succeeded in getting away again undiscovered. I was then told the great secret, and we all set out on our expedition. This secret was a convent legend, handed down for more than two centuries, — founded, perhaps, on reality, but which certainly at this late day was only perpetuated by our lively imaginations. We were to find and deliver " the victim." There was somewhere a prisoner — some said several prisoners — confined in a

cell contrived in the thickness of the walls,
or else incarcerated in a deep dungeon beneath the vaults of the immense subterranean passages that extended not only under
the whole monastery but beneath a great
part of that quarter of the city. There was
really a great underground labyrinth, which
we never fully explored, and from which we
emerged into different parts of the cellars
of the vast convent buildings. We said to
each other that these passages must be
connected with the excavations that under-
lie a great part of Paris and the surround-
ing country as far as Vincennes. From
the convent cellars perhaps we could get
into the catacombs, the quarries, the Palais
des Thermes. In short, to us it was the
entrance to a whole world of darkness, terror, and mystery, — a gulf under our very
feet, closed with iron doors; and our exploring expeditions were as fraught with
imaginary peril as the descent into hell of
Æneas or Dante. The danger was the
great temptation, to which we yielded
with delight, in spite of the insurmountable difficulties of the enterprise and the
condign punishment that no doubt awaited
our detection.

There was a main entrance wide open at the foot of the cellar stairs leading from the kitchen; but the lay sisters were always near at hand, and we were persuaded that there were many other ways of getting in. According to us, every walled-up door, every dark corner, every wall that sounded hollow, might be in mysterious connection with these places; and we tried unweariedly to find an opening, even under the roofs. I had read Mrs. Radcliffe, and my companions had a store of Scotch and Irish legends that would make your hair stand on end; the convent, too, had its own stories of ghostly apparitions and mysterious noises. All that, and the undying hope of discovering "the victim," stimulated the girls to a wild enthusiasm; and they were easily persuaded that they heard sighs and groans issuing from the ground under their feet, or from fissures in the doors and walls.

So I set out on my first expedition, thrilled with the expectation of finding the long-lost captive. It might have quenched our enthusiasm to consider that she was no longer young, — two hundred years old more or less; but we never stopped to think about that. We sought, we called aloud, we thought of her unceasingly, and never despaired of success.

That night we directed our steps to the most ruinous part of the building, — very mysterious for a nocturnal exploration, — and cautiously walked along a narrow shelf on the brink of what we supposed to be a deep cellar, without any apparent outlet. A mouldy wooden railing guarded the edge, and stairs, with a baluster, led down to this unknown region ; but an oaken door at the head of these stairs closed the entrance, and we found it was padlocked. To circumvent this obstacle we managed to squeeze between the rails, and walking on the outer edge of the worm-eaten baluster, we reached the other side of the door at the head of the stairs. Below us yawned a dark abyss ; we had only one little coil of wax taper, called a " rat de cave," that shed a faint light on the upper steps of this mysterious stairway, and it seemed a great risk ; but Isabella led the way like a heroine, Mary followed with the practised ease and agility of a professor of gymnastics, and we all imitated her, more or less clumsily, and never thought of turning back.

In a moment we were at the foot of the flight, but discovered, with more joy I think than real disappointment, that there was no getting out of this square cellar but the way by which we had come. There was no door, no window, no apparent or assignable use for this large space absolutely without egress. What could be the object of a staircase to get down into such a place? we said; and why was there a solid padlocked door to close the entrance? We divided the taper, and each one searched for herself. There might be a secret trap-door, leading to a passage, under one of the wooden stairs. While some examined the steps, and tried to pry the old boards apart, others sounded the walls, hoping to find a crack, a button, or a hidden ring, — some Radcliffian invention to lift a stone or move a sliding panel that would prove the entrance to mysterious and unknown regions. But we discovered nothing of the kind; the rough, whitewashed wall presented an unbroken surface, the floor sounded dead under our feet, we could find no flagstone to lift, and the staircase concealed no secret passage. But Isabella would not give up; in the farthest corner under the stairs she was sure that the wall sounded hollow. We all tried it, and were convinced that it was really so.

" That is it ! " we cried. " There must be the entrance to the secret dungeon, — to the sepulchre of living victims."

We all listened intently, but heard nothing. Isabella, however, declared that she could plainly distinguish low moans, and clanking of chains. What was to be done ?

" Nothing is easier," said Mary. " We must break through this masonry ; all together we can certainly make a hole in this wall."

So we went to work with a good will, some knocking with sticks of wood, others scraping away with shovels and tongs, without once stopping to think of the danger of bringing the old wall down on our heads. Fortunately we could not accomplish much, because if we dealt heavy blows, the noise would betray us, — so we could do nothing but poke and scratch ; but we had succeeded in making quite a pile of rubbish when the bell rang for prayers. We had barely time to make our perilous ascent, put out our lights, and grope our way back to the schoolroom, appointing a rendezvous for the next night at the same hour. It was agreed that no one should wait for the others who might be kept away by punishment, or called back as they were going out. Each one should do her best to make a breach in the wall. There was no danger of the heap of rubbish attracting attention, for the place seemed given up to mice and spiders.

We helped one another to brush off the dust and lime with which we were covered, hurried through the cloisters, and got back to our schoolroom just as prayers were beginning. I do not remember being punished that time; but not infrequently we escaped with impunity. Miss D—— used to knit of an evening, talking all the time, and squabbling with Mary Eyre. The room was imperfectly lighted, and I do not think her sight was very good. However that may be, with all her love of espionage, she was not very discerning; and we often succeeded in eluding her vigilance. In fact, once outside the schoolroom door, it would have been hard to find us in the great rambling convent, and she was probably afraid of a scandal if she divulged our frequent absences, — for which they might hold her accountable; the fact would have been a discredit to her discipline: and we cared as little for the penitential night-cap as we did at last for the lavish abuse of this delightful person. The Superior, politic and indulgent, was not inclined to keep us from going out on holidays, and she alone decided those questions; so that upon the whole we had a great deal of liberty, in spite of the bad temper of our schoolmistress.

The pursuit of the great secret, the search for the victim, was continued all the winter; and we made a considerable breach in the wall before coming to heavy beams that brought us to a full stop. Then we sought elsewhere, dug in twenty different places, without any success, but with unfailing hope. One day we took a fancy to seek an entrance to the subterranean world of our dreams by descending from the roof, where there were a great many mansard windows lighting undiscovered regions. In one of these garrets was a small room for piano practice, — one of the thirty or more scattered about the establishment. We all were ex-

pected to practise an hour at least every
day, and sometimes we were sent to the
garret for this purpose, — thus affording a
good opportunity for adventures by day as
well as by night. We agreed to meet in
one of these out-of-the-way rooms, and
thence start as fancy led in search of the
unknown. From the attic where I was
supposed to be practising scales, I could
see a wide expanse of roofs, sheds, and pent-
houses, all covered with moss-grown tiles
and diversified by tumble-down chimneys.
This was a fine field for new exploring expeditions; so out we went on the roofs,
jumping down from the window to a gutter,
six feet below us, connecting two gables.
To scramble up these gables, encounter
others, leap like cats from one steep roof to
another, was more dangerous than difficult;
and the risk only added to the delightful
excitement.

For more than an hour we had gone
on in this way in our lofty gymnasium
overlooking the gardens, — dodging behind a chimney whenever we caught sight
of the black veil of a sister who might
have looked up, — when all at once we
stopped and asked one another how we were

ever going to get back. Jumping up was
a different thing from jumping down ; and
in some places we should certainly have
needed a ladder. Moreover, we had no idea
where we were. At last we recognized the
window of a private pupil, — Sidonie Mac-
donald, daughter of the celebrated general,—
and we could get there by one more jump,
longer than any we had yet undertaken. I
was in too much of a hurry, and caught my
heel in the sash of a skylight over a gallery,
breaking half a dozen panes of glass, that
fell with a crash thirty feet below into a
court close to the entrance of the kitchens.
I should have fallen through also, but
fortunately came down sidewise, and escaped with skinning my knees, which bled
profusely.

Great excitement ensued among the lay
sisters, who came running out. Lying low
aloft, we heard the resounding voice of
Sister Theresa abusing the cats and accusing " Whisky," the favorite tabby of Mother
Alippe, of fighting with the others and
breaking all the window-glass in the convent. Sister Marie took up the cudgels for
Whisky, and Sister Helen was sure that a
chimney had been blown down on the

roof. Hearing them talk in this way threw us into uncontrollable fits of laughter : we knew that they were coming upstairs to investigate ; but though in danger of being detected in the unpardonable sin of scrambling over the roofs, we could not have moved to save our lives. One girl was stretched out at full length in a gutter, another had lost her comb, and I had just discovered that one of my shoes had gone through the opening and fallen at the kitchen door. In spite of my knees, I was choking with laughter, and could only point to my shoeless foot and explain the situation by signs; then there was a new explosion of laughter.

But the alarm had been given, and we heard the sisters coming. This sobered us, and gave us time to reflect that where we were it was impossible for them to see us unless they mounted by a ladder to the broken skylight, or followed in the way we had come over the roofs; and we were perfectly sure that the nuns would not do that. Once conscious of the superior advantages of our position, we began to mew vigorously, so that Whisky and his companions might be accused and convicted in our stead; and then we all climbed through Sidonie's window, without, however, meeting with a very cordial reception. The poor child, practising conscientiously, had paid no attention to the feline howls that saluted her ears. She was delicate and nervous, very gentle and quiet, quite incapable of understanding what pleasure there could be in such expeditions as ours. When she heard us all bouncing through the window, to which her back was turned, she jumped up, and screamed with terror. We could not stop to explain, fearing that her cries would bring the nuns to her assistance; so we darted through the room and out of the door, while, trembling all over, with affrighted eyes she saw the strange procession rush by, without guessing what it meant, or recognizing one of us in her bewilderment. In a moment we had scattered: one ran up to the room whence we started, and played with all her might on the piano; another went a long way round to reach the schoolroom; my anxiety was to recover my shoe, and I was fortunate enough to find it before that incriminating piece of evidence had been noticed, or brought forward by any one. Whisky was

formally accused, and bore all the blame, —
but not all the penalty, for my knees were
very painful for several days. I said nothing about it, however, and our nightly expeditions went on as usual.

IV.

B UT for this constant excitement, I do
not believe that I could have remained
in the convent. The fare was very good ;
but we suffered cruelly from cold, and the
winter was exceptionally severe. The first
half of the day I was literally benumbed.
Our dormitory was under the mansard roof,
and it was so cold there that often I could
not sleep, and heard the clock strike hour
after hour. At six the two maids, Josepha
and Marie Anne, came pitilessly to wake
us up ; and washing and dressing by candle-
light in the morning has always seemed to
me forlorn. We often broke the ice for
our ablutions, to get at water that did not
wash. Then we had chilblains, and it
was dreadful to squeeze our swollen, sometimes bleeding feet into tight shoes. We
heard mass by candle-light, shivering in
our seats, or falling asleep on our knees in
the attitude of devotion. At seven we
breakfasted on a bit of bread and a cup of

tea, and at last in the schoolroom saw the light of day, and a little fire in the stove; but as I said, it was often noon before I thawed out. I had severe colds, and sharp pains in all my limbs; and it was fifteen years before I fully recovered from the effect of these hardships. But my friend Mary could not tolerate complaining. Strong as a boy herself, she scorned want of endurance in others; and in much suffering I learned the hard lesson of not indulging in self-pity.

When my grandmother was about to leave Paris she asked permission to have me with her for two or three consecutive Thursdays. The Superior did not dare to acknowledge that I had bad marks from all the teachers without exception, that I was making no progress, and that the night-cap was my habitual head-dress. If she had done so, my grandmother might have said that since I was wasting my time, I had better go home; therefore little notice was taken of my idleness or misdemeanors.

I expected to enjoy these holidays far more than I really did. I had become accustomed to living in common with other girls, and to passing comparatively unnoticed; and

4

at home they made too much of me, asked
me too many questions, said I was changed,
dull, or absent-minded. When evening
came, and they took me back to the convent, the first impression was painful; the
contrast was too great, — coming from the
warm, perfumed, well-lighted parlor, to the
cold, dark cloister, with its bare walls; from
my grandmother's fond caresses, to the
glum salutation of the porter and the nun
at the turning-box. I shivered as I hurried
through the corridors paved with tombstones; but once past the cloisters, I was
under the spell. Vanloo's madonna seemed
to smile down on me; I was not devout,
but the bluish light of her little lamp
always threw me into a sweet, vague
revery. I heard Mary call me impatiently;
the stupid girls thronged about me, asking
what I had seen and what I had done
through the day.

" Is n't it horrid to come back? " they said.

I did not answer; for I could not tell
why I liked the convent life better than
living with my family.

On the eve of my grandmother's departure a great storm burst upon me. Although I was no talker, I wrote with great

ease, and delighted in keeping a journal, in which our daily misdemeanors and the punishments inflicted by Miss D—— were duly recorded in a sarcastic style. This was regularly sent to my grandmother, who seemed very much amused, and, far from scolding me, never once inculcated submission or cajolery, — certainly not hypocrisy. It was customary to leave all the letters to be sent away every night on a chest in the Superior's ante-chamber. Those not addressed to relatives must be left open; but parents' letters were always sealed, and it was understood that the seal was to be respected. It would have been very easy for me to send these effusions by the servants, who often brought me things, or came to ask how I was; but it never entered my head to doubt the honor of the Superior. She had said in so many words before me that she never opened letters written to parents, and I believed her.

It appeared that the volume and frequency of my letters had aroused her suspicion, and that she had deliberately unsealed and suppressed my satires, doing this repeatedly before denouncing me, so that she might become well acquainted

with my ideas and statements about Miss
D ——— . If the reverend mother had been
wise and kindly, she might have availed
herself of this discovery, — reproving me,
but dismissing the teacher. A really good
woman, however, never could have set
such a trap for an unsuspecting child, or
have violated a confidence she had herself authorized. Madame Canning showed
the letters to Miss D ———, who naturally
enough did not think my unflattering portrait a very good likeness. The hatred
already provoked by my invincible obsti-
nacy, as well as by the calm suavity of
my manners, flamed out. She called me
an abominable liar, a free thinker, a vile
informer, a serpent. The Superior then
confronted her with me; but I remained
unrepentant and mute, till Madame Canning graciously volunteered not to let my
grandmother know, and to keep silence
in regard to these infamous letters. I felt
keenly the duplicity of such a proceeding,
and told her that I had a rough draft of
each one of my letters, that my grandmother should have it, and that I should
maintain then and now the truth of my
assertions; moreover, that since I could

not depend upon assurances that had been made me, I should ask my grandmother to take me away from the convent.

It cannot be said that the Superior was destitute of good qualities ; but her conduct was not calculated to inspire respect, when, pouring out the vials of her wrath on my head, with a torrent of abuse she ordered me to leave the room instantly. Though a woman of the world, who could be queenly in her manner at times, she certainly was not ladylike when she flew into a rage. Perhaps, however, as a foreigner, she did not appreciate the full value of the expressions she used, and I did not know enough English to be rebuked in that language. Miss D—— shut her eyes, and looked down with a hypocritical expression, as if she were a saint listening to the voice of God in her soul, pitying me, and keeping silence in mercy.

An hour afterwards the Superior entered the refectory, followed by a train of attendant nuns. After inspecting the table, she stopped directly in front of me, and opening her handsome dark eyes very wide, said impressively, —

"Try and speak the truth!"

The good girls shuddered and crossed themselves, the stupid ones whispered to one another and stared at me; and when dinner was over I was eagerly questioned to know what it meant.

"It means," I said, "that next week I shall not be here."

I was very angry, but deeply grieved; for I did not want to leave the convent, and break up my precious friendships.

My grandmother arrived, was closeted with the Superior, who, sure that I would tell everything, made up her mind at last to relinquish my letters, characterizing them as a shameless tissue of falsehoods. I rather think that she had the worst of it, and that my grandmother told her plainly what she thought of such an abuse of confidence, defending me, and declaring that she should take me away at once.

However that may be, I know that when I was summoned to the Superior's parlor both ladies were trying to be very grave and quiet, and both looked very much excited. My grandmother kissed me affectionately, and reproached me for nothing but my idleness, and the time I had wasted in childish mischief. Then the Superior said that it was decided that I was to leave the lower division, where my intimacy with Mary had proved so prejudicial, and enter immediately the higher class.

This piece of good news — a change for the better in reality — was announced in a very severe tone of voice. She hoped that since I should now be separated from Miss D ——, I would cease to satirize her, and told me that I must at once break off my relations with Mary. She trusted that this enforced separation might be of use to both of us.

I assured her that I was perfectly willing to let Miss D —— alone, but that I should never promise not to love Mary. Of course we must be separated, since we could only meet now in the garden at recess.

My grandmother went off to Nohant, very well satisfied with the result of this affair. I was promoted to the upper class, where Sophia and Isabella had already preceded me. I vowed to Mary a friendship for life and death; but I had not heard the last of the dreadful Miss D ——.

V.

I MUST not leave the lower class without mentioning two girls whom I loved
very much, although they were not "diables," — Valentine de Gouy and Louise de
la Rochejaquelein.

Valentine was a mere child, — if I remember rightly, — about nine or ten years old;
and as she was small and delicate, she
did not seem much older than Mary Eyre
and Helen Kelly, the two " babies " of the
class.   But she was so intelligent that her
companionship was as agreeable as Sophia's
or Isabella's.   With a marvellous facility
of acquiring, she was as far advanced in
her studies as many of the larger girls; and
she was very interesting, too, — full of can-
dor and kindness.   My bed was next to
Valentine's in the dormitory, and I liked
to take care of her at night as if she had
been my child.

The other friend, who soon rejoined me
in the upper class, was Louise de la Roche-

jaquelein, daughter of the Marchioness de la Rochejaquelein who wrote an interesting history of the first Vendean war, — a book that does equal credit to the·head and the heart of its author. Louise had inherited from her mother, with that heart and head, the courage and intolerance of the old Chouans, as well as the poetic nobleness of that warlike peasantry among whom she had been brought up. I had read Madame de la Rochejaquelein's book, published not long before, and though I had no sympathy with Louise's royalist prejudices, I avoided all dispute, feeling a profound respect for her religious inheritance, and great interest in her vivid descriptions of the manners and scenery of " Le Bocage."

I visited her once, a few years later, and saw her mother. I do not remember exactly where they lived, but it was a great hotel of the Faubourg Saint Germain. I arrived modestly in a hack, — an equipage suited to my means and habits, — and alighted in the street, for the door of the court was not swung open to hired carriages. The porter, an old family servant, tried to stop me as I entered ; but I said,

"Excuse me, but I have come to see Madame de la Rochejaquelein."

"You!" he said, surveying me from head to foot, with evident contempt for my plain street dress. "Well, then, come in;" and he shrugged his shoulders, as if to say, "The family receives Tom, Dick, and Harry."

I tried to close the door behind me, but it was too heavy; so I left it ajar, not wishing to soil my gloves, and I was already half-way upstairs when the old Cerberus called after me, —

"Your door!"

"What door?"

"The street door."

"Oh, excuse me! that is your door, not mine," I answered, laughing.

He went off, grumbling, to shut it, and I kept on my way, wondering if the illustrious lackeys of my old friend would treat me in the same manner.

Seeing a great many of these gentlemen in the antechamber, I perceived that there was company, and sent in my card to Louise; for I was in Paris only for a few days, and she had expressed a wish to see me. She came out directly, and carried me off to the drawing-room with all her old gayety and cordiality. In the corner where she made me sit down by her there were only young persons, — her sisters and their friends. The older guests were clustered round her mother, who occupied an arm-chair a little apart from the rest. I was terribly disappointed to find that the heroine of La Vendée was a common-looking, red-faced woman. On her right stood a Vendean peasant, who had left his village probably for the first time, to see her or to see Paris. He had been dining with the family. Undoubtedly he was an old re-tainer, perhaps a hero of the last Vendée; for he seemed too young to have been in the first war, and Louise only said, in an-swer to my inquiry, " He is one of our good peasants." Coarsely dressed in jacket and trousers, with a white scarf on his arm, he carried a venerable rapier, that was always getting between his legs, and made him look like a constable in a country pro-cession. Altogether he was not at all my ideal partisan, — half shepherd and half brigand, — and he had a way of saying, every minute, " Madame la Marquise," that displeased me very much.

But I admired the high-bred kindness and simplicity of the old lady's manners : she was almost blind; and as she sat there surrounded by a bevy of beautiful women, all showing her profound respect, I said to myself, " Not one of them all has for that white hair and those dimmed blue eyes half the veneration, perhaps, that I feel for her in my heart of hearts, — a secret homage, more to be appreciated because it is the spontaneous tribute of a girl who is neither a devotee nor a royalist." Her conversation seemed to me more sensible than witty.

When the peasant took leave, he shook hands, put his hat hard on his head, and strode out of the room ; but no one even smiled.

Louise and her sisters were as simple in their dress as in their manners, which were plain, sometimes almost abrupt. They had no fancy work, but spun flax, peasant-fashion, with a distaff. It all seemed charming to me then, and perhaps it was so. Louise, I am sure, was perfectly simple and natural; but there was something incongruous about it. The surroundings of a Vendean Châtelaine did not harmonize very well

with such rural occupations. A beautiful
drawing-room, brilliantly lighted; an admir-
ing crowd of noble, well-dressed ladies and
ceremonious aristocrats; an antechamber
full of lackeys; a porter who almost insulted
visitors who came in hired carriages,—
there was a discordant note that made you
feel the insuperable difficulty of a public
and legitimate union of the people with
the nobility.

VI.

I HAVE kept the elementary school-
books we used in the lower class, the
spelling-book, the "Garden of the Soul,"
etc.   They are scribbled over with mot-
toes and rebuses, and best of all with
the dialogues that we kept up surrepti-
tiously during enforced silence, — a very
common punishment.

The cover of the book we were using —
passed along under the table — kept the conversation going at such times; and we also
had letters, cut out of pasteboard, slipped
on a string from one end of the schoolroom
to the other.   Words were rapidly formed
in this way, and even a girl set apart by
herself in a corner, for some misdemeanor,
was easily kept informed of what was
going on.

Sometimes we improvised written confessions and examinations of conscience
for the little girls, of which the following

is a specimen; but I do not remember who wrote it, nor for whom it was intended.

CONFESSION OF ———.

Alas! dear Father Villèle, I very often get ink on my hands. Sometimes I snuff the candle with my fingers; and when I eat too many beans, I suffer from indigestion, — as I was taught to say in the fashionable world where I was brought up. I have shocked the young ladies of the class by my untidiness. I have looked as stupid as an owl, and I have forgotten to think of anything in particular, more than two hundred times a day. I have gone to sleep at catechism, and I have snored at mass. I have said that you were not handsome. I have let my taper drip on Mother Alippe's veil, and I meant to do it. This last week I have said *s* for *t* and *t* for *s* more than fifteen times in French, and thirty times in English. I have burned my shoes at the stove and made a bad smell in the schoolroom. It is my fault, my fault, my very great fault, etc.

Such nonsense was not very impious; but we were severely reprimanded and punished if Miss D—— found any compositions of this kind. Mother Alippe pretended to be angry, inflicted some slight punishment, and confiscated the papers, with which I suspect she sometimes amused the nuns in the work-room.

It does not take much to set a parcel of
little girls laughing, and panic is as conta-
gious as laughter.   A timid child would
scream at a spider, and then the whole class
shrieked in concert, without knowing why.
One evening at prayer-time, — I cannot tell
what happened ; no one ever found out.
But one of the pupils screamed ; her neighbor jumped up, the next left her seat, and
there was immediately a general stampede.
We rushed out of the room, knocking down
the chairs and candles, overturning the
benches and tables, tumbling over one another as we fled along the cloisters, drag-
ging with us the teachers, who screamed
and ran just as we did.   It was a whole
hour before calm was restored, and an in-
vestigation made ; but no cause was ever
discovered.

In spite of all this feverish excitement,
I suffered so much physically and morally
in the lower class that I remember the day
when I entered the older girls' schoolroom,
and belonged there, as one of the happiest
in my life.

I have always been dependent on light,
finding dark places depressing.   The
schoolroom for the second division was

spacious, with five or six large windows, almost all opening on the garden. It was warmed by a bright open fire, and a good stove. Then, too, it was early spring, and the great candelabras of the horse-chestnuts were almost in bloom. It seemed like paradise.

The presiding genius of the place, who went by the name of " the Countess," was very much ridiculed by the girls. She was really very eccentric, and almost as absentminded as Miss D——; but she was a good woman. Her own apartment on the ground floor, opening on a garden, was only separated from our domain by some beds of vegetables; so that from her window, when she was not on duty, she could see what we were about. But it interested her much more to watch from the schoolroom what was going on in her own apartment. There at her window, or out in front at her door, lived, climbed, scratched, and screeched in the sunshine the only object of her idolatry, — a shabby-looking gray parrot, — an ill-natured old thing, constantly insulted and despised by the girls. We were very wrong to behave so, however, for we certainly owed a great deal to Jacquot. Thanks to him, the Countess often left us to our own devices. Perched on his stick, in full view from her seat in the schoolroom, Jacquot uttered piercing cries whenever he was not particularly amusing himself. The Countess would run directly to the window, and if a cat were seen prowling about near his perch, or if, tired of the sameness of life, the discontented bird had started off for a pleasure trip in the lilac-bushes, she forgot everything else, and rushed madly through the cloisters across the garden, to reclaim, scold, and caress the dear delinquent. Meantime, we danced about on the tables, or, following Jacquot's bad example, went off to amuse ourselves in garret or cellar.

The Countess was forty or fifty years old, unmarried, of noble birth (as she constantly reminded us), and probably uneducated,— for she never gave any lessons, but was a sort of superintendent. Though she was undeniably tiresome and ridiculous, she was naturally kind, and perfectly respectable. Yet some of us disliked her so much, and treated her so badly, that we forced her to be severe at times. She was always kind to me, and I am ashamed to say that I laughed with the others at her lofty airs, at the black poke bonnet she never took off, at the green shawl constantly pulled up on her shoulders, and at her frequent lapses in speaking, — which we never allowed to pass unnoticed, and pitilessly reproduced in our own conversation. This mimicry delighted us, and she never found it out. I ought to have taken her part, for she often espoused mine when I was in disgrace; but children are proverbially ungrateful. La Fontaine says, "This age is pitiless." The right to ridicule seems to it an inalienable right.

Our second superintendent was a very austere nun, — Madame Anne Frances. She was aged, thin, and pale, with a great Roman nose; her strongly marked face was full of character, and she looked like an old Dominican. She scolded a great deal, upbraided us too much, and was decidedly not a favorite. I neither liked nor disliked her, and she seemed indifferent to me, — though I never could see that she preferred any of the girls. We strongly suspected her of being philosophical, because she was so much interested in astronomy. In some ways she was very different from the other sisters. For instance, instead of communing, as they did, every day, she only approached the sacraments on great festivals. Her reprimands never did us any good; they were nothing but threats, uttered in such bad French that it was hard not to laugh outright. She punished a great deal; and when she happened to be jocose, her pleasantries were coarse and offensive. She certainly was not devout, — not even pious for a nun.

Our principal was Madame Eugénie, — a tall woman with a beautiful figure and noble bearing, very graceful and stately. Rosy and wrinkled, like most middle-aged nuns, her pretty face was disfigured by a haughty, almost scornful expression, that repelled one on first acquaintance. We found her more than strict, — severe, and sometimes caustic in her remarks; and she allowed herself to be so unduly influenced by her personal antipathies that she never became popular with the girls. Her manners were so cold and reserved that I never knew any one but myself with whom she had affectionate relations; but I was really fond of her, and this was the way our friendship originated.

Three days after my promotion to the

first class I happened to meet Miss D——
as I was going into the garden at recreation,
and she looked at me savagely. I returned
her stare with my habitual coolness. She
had felt herself humiliated by my advance-
ment, and was perfectly furious.

"You are very lofty," she said; "you do
not even deign to speak to me."

"Good morning, madam. How do you
do?"

"You need not be so impertinent; I can
make you feel who I am."

"I hope not, madam; I have nothing
more to do with you."

"Wait and see!" and she walked away
with a threatening gesture.

It was the hour of recess; everybody was
in the garden; and I took this opportunity
of getting some copy-books that I had left
in a closet adjoining the schoolroom. This
closet (where they kept writing-desks, ink-
stands, and large pitchers full of water for
washing the floor) served also as a prison
for the little ones, — Mary Eyre and Company. I had been there a few minutes,
trying to find my books, when Miss
D—— suddenly appeared before me like
Tisiphone.

" I am very glad to find you here," she said. " Now you shall ask my pardon for the impertinent way you looked at me just now."

" No, madam," I replied; " I was not impertinent, and I shall not ask your pardon."

" Very well, then I shall punish you as I do the little girls; you shall stay shut up here till you change your mind."

" You have no right to do so; you have no longer any authority over me."

" Try, then, and get out."

" Very well, I am going out now; " and taking advantage of her astonishment, I walked out of the closet.

Transported with rage, she rushed at me, grasped me in her arms, and pushed me in again. In all my life I never saw anything more repulsive than this pious fury. Half in fun and half in earnest, I kept her off and held her against the wall, — nothing more, — till I saw that she was going to strike me, and then I raised my clinched fist. She turned very pale; and when I felt that she was giving way, I contemptuously released her, satisfied with having shown my physical and moral superiority. Taking advantage at once of my magnanimity, she returned to the charge and pushed me with all her might. My foot hit a great jug of water, that overturned as I fell into the closet, where Miss D—— locked me in, pouring out a volley of abuse. The situation was not pleasant: I was literally in a cold bath, — for the closet was small and the pitcher enormous ; the water came up to my ankles. But I could not help laughing when I heard her mutter: " The perverse, miserable child ! She has made me so angry that I shall have to confess all over again. I have lost my absolution."

When she had gone, I gathered my wits together, climbed upon a shelf out of reach of the water, tore a blank leaf out of a copy-book, found pen and ink, and wrote a note to Madame Eugénie something like this :

" MADAME, — I recognize no authority but your own. Miss D—— has just shut me up by main force. Please come and let me out."

Then I waited for a messenger, and presently one of the girls came to the school-room. Seeing me looking out of the transom, she was frightened, and turned to run away ; but I called her back, and begged her to take my letter to Madame Eugénie, who

was in the garden. A few minutes after,
Madame appeared, followed by Miss D——,
took me by the hand and led me away without saying a word. Miss D—— held her
peace too. When I was alone in the cloister with Madame Eugénie, I threw my arms
about her and kissed her affectionately. She
was not given to caresses, and I had never
seen any one kiss her before; but she was
evidently not displeased with my impulsive
action, and seemed affected by my warm
embrace, — like a woman who does not know
what it is to be loved, and yet yearns for
affection. She questioned me skilfully;
and without appearing to heed my answers
particularly, she did not lose a word or an expression of my face. Persuaded at last that
I spoke the truth, she grasped my hand
tenderly, and told me to go back to the
garden.

The Archbishop of Paris was coming in
a few days to confirm some of the girls who
had had their first communion but had not
partaken of the sacrament. They were to
make their "retreat" together in a room
presided over by Miss D——, who was also
the reader, and made the religious exhorta-
tions. That very day I was sent for as

one of the number, but she refused to receive me, and ordered me to make my "retreat" in a room by myself somewhere.

Then Madame Eugénie took my part openly.

"Is she so pestilential as that?" she said ironically. "Then she had better come to me in my cell."

She took me by the hand, and we went out, followed by Mother Alippe. While I made myself at home in the cell, the two nuns stayed outside in the corridor, and I overheard their conversation, which was carried on in English. Perhaps they did not know that I could understand them as well as I did.

"Tell me," began Madame Eugénie, "is this child really so abominable?"

"She is not abominable at all," answered Mother Alippe. "She is a good enough child; that woman makes all the trouble. 'T is true that she is a 'diable,' as they call them. I see that makes you laugh; I have always understood that you have a weakness for 'les diables.'"

"Good!" said I to myself; "that is worth remembering."

Madame Eugénie went on: "But she is

such a wild child that perhaps she had better not be confirmed at present; she is hardly sober-minded enough.   Wait till she has sown her wild oats; and meantime let us keep her out of the way of this woman, who owes her a grudge.   You agree that the child belongs now to me, and that you have no longer any right to control her?"

"No other right but that of Christian charity," said Mother Alippe: "but don't disturb yourself; Miss D—— is clearly in the wrong, and must stop where she is."

Then they went off, — as I supposed to find the Superior, explain the matter to her, and confer perhaps also with Miss D——.

While I was awaiting their return, — safely ensconced in the cell of my protec- tress, — our dear sympathetic Poulette came in to console me.   That was the name we children had given to the sister of Mother Alippe, — Madam Mary Austin, the treas- urer of the community.   We idolized her; for not having any official relation with the pupils, and consequently no responsibility, she took it upon herself to spoil us contin- ually, — administering, however, a good-

humored scolding now and then for our
frolics. She kept a store of dainties that
we could buy, and they were often given
to the girls who were out of money, —
opening accounts never closed by debtor
or creditor. This kind soul had no gloom
or austerity in her piety. Always gay,
we hugged and kissed, even teased her,
without ever making her angry. Now she
came to comfort me in my misfortunes,
with such ardent sympathy and exaggerated sense of my wrongs that she might
have done me harm if I had not really
longed to live in peace with every one.

After we had chatted an hour or more,
the door opened, and who should come in
but Miss D——! Evidently she had been
taken to task by the Superior, or her confessor ; for she was as sweet as honey, and
I was stupefied by her novel, caressing
ways. She announced that I was not to
be confirmed before next year, because I
was not thought to be in a proper frame of
mind to receive the sacrament, — adding
that Madame Eugénie was coming to tell
me herself, but that she had obtained permission to do so, because she wanted to be
reconciled, — to make her peace with me

before going into "retreat" with the other girls.

"Come, now," she said; "acknowledge that you have been wrong, and give me your hand!"

"Willingly," I answered. " I will do anything that you ask kindly and pleasantly."

Then she kissed me. I did not like that; but the storm had blown over, and I never had any trouble with her again. The next year, after my conversion, I made my "retreat" under her auspices. She was very amiable, and complimented me on my change of heart. She read to us a great deal, explaining and commenting with a certain rude eloquence that was sometimes magnetic. At first her manner of reading seemed bombastic; but after a while it was impressive. I remember nothing more about her from this time. I forgave her sincerely, and never regretted it; but I must say that we should have been infinitely better, and far happier, if the nuns had devoted themselves to our education, instead of leaving it in the hands of such women.

VII.

ONE of the oldest nuns whom I remember was Madame Anne Augustine. She was so aged and infirm that we used to say one had plenty of time to learn one's lessons going upstairs behind her to recitation. She never spoke French, and had a very severe and solemn expression. I do not believe that she ever said a word to any one of us. The story ran that after a very serious illness she had to wear a silver stomach. This was a current convent tradition, and we were silly enough to accept and repeat it. We even persuaded ourselves sometimes that we could hear it click as she walked; and this old nun, mended with metal, who never spoke to us, who did not know the name of a single girl, and who gave us a startled look as we passed, became in our imaginations a very mysterious and rather a dreadful being. We trembled as we bowed to her. She returned our salutations silently, and passed

on like a spectre. We used to declare that
she must have died two hundred years before, and that it was her ghost we saw keeping up the habit of walking about.

Madame Marie Xavier was the most
beautiful person in the convent, —tall, slight,
and well-formed. She was always as white
as a sheet, and as gloomy as the grave, —saying that she was very ill, and only hoped to
die. She was the only nun I ever saw in
despair because she had pronounced the
final vows; but she made no secret of the
fact, and passed her time in sighs and tears.
The law does not sanction such vows nowadays: but she did not dare, apparently, to
break them, since she had solemnly sworn;
and while she was not philosophical enough
to do this, she was not pious enough to
become resigned to her fate. Faltering,
restless, and wretched, she seemed more im-
passioned than loving; for she often gave
way to fits of anger, as if utterly worn out
and exasperated. We talked a great deal
about her. Some of us thought that she
had taken the veil on account of a disappointment, and that she still cared for her
lover; others said that she hated him,
and that her heart was full of rage and re-

sentment; while a few accused her of having an unhappy temper, and of chafing under the authority of the older nuns. Although it was all kept from us as much as possible, we could not help seeing that she lived apart, that the sisters seemed to condemn her, and that she was on cool terms with all the others, whose dislike she returned. Yet she communed daily, and remained, I believe, ten years in the convent. Not long after I went away I heard that she had broken her vows, and departed; but no one knew how it came to pass. What was the end of her sorrowful life? Did she find the object of her passion free and repentant; or did she never really have a passion? Did she go back to the world, or enter another convent, to end her days in penitence and mourning; or did she die of a broken heart? None of us ever knew. The sisters explained her absence, saying that the doctors declared that she must live in a different climate and change her manner of life; but it was easy to see, by their constrained smiles, that there was a mystery about it.

Another beautiful girl, — Miss Croft, — who entered as a postulant while I was at

the convent, after my departure followed
the example of Madame Marie Xavier, and
left the community, — before taking the
black veil, however.

Miss Hurst — who took the final vows
during my stay, and who did it very deliberately, without repenting afterwards — was
my English teacher, and I passed an hour
every day in her cell. She explained all the
difficulties of the language clearly and pa-
tiently, and I became very fond of her, —
with reason, for she was extremely kind to
me, even when I was a " diable." Her convent name was Maria Winifred; and I
never read Shakespeare or Byron in the
original without thanking her in my heart.

Sister Anne Joseph was the gentlest and
most affectionate little creature that ever
breathed, — without a particle of English
stiffness or Roman Catholic caution. She
was always kissing us, and calling us by the
most endearing names ; but her talk was as
incoherent as her ideas, and she chattered
away without really saying anything. It
may be that she had so much to say that
she could not express it, even in her own
language. There did not seem to be so
much absence, as utter confusion of ideas.

Her thoughts got ahead of her speech; and then she used the wrong word, or left a phrase unfinished, so that you had to guess the end while she was rattling on with another. Her actions were like her talk; she tried to do forty things at once, and naturally never did one well. Her gentleness and sweet temper seemed to fit her for the place she had in the infirmary; but unfortunately, when she was flurried she could not tell her right hand from her left, or doses of medicine from outward applications, and made sad confusion with patients and prescriptions. In a great hurry to get something in the pharmacy, she would run upstairs when she should have run down, and *vice versa*. Her whole life was passed in trying to correct her mistakes. "As good as an angel and as silly as a goose," they used to say of her; and I sometimes thought that the other nuns were needlessly severe, and laughed too much at her misfortunes. Once she complained of having rats in her cell, and was told that they must have come out of her own brain. When she had done something hopelessly absurd she would get completely bewildered, and shed tears in despair. Poor little Sister Anne Joseph!

6

You did well in your trouble to turn to God, who never rejects the offering of a loving heart; and I thank him for enabling me to feel the beauty of your perfect simplicity and tenderness! Scorn such if you will, — you who often find unselfish goodness like hers in the world!

I have kept the nun whom I loved most dearly for the last picture in this portrait gallery. Madame Marie Alicia was the best, the most attractive, and the most intelligent of all the women, old and young, who inhabited this English Augustinian convent. When I first knew her, she could not have been thirty years old; and she was still very handsome, though her mouth was rather small, and her nose too large. But those great blue eyes, with their long black lashes, were more tender, more limpid, and more truthful than any other eyes I ever saw in my life. In them all her generous, candid, motherly soul, — all her pure, lofty aspirations, — lay mirrored. In mystic language they might have been called "wells of purity." Even now, when I awake in the night from some bad dream, — that haunts me even when wide awake, — I recall Madame Alicia's eyes;

and their pure rays always put the phan-
toms to flight. It is no affectionate exaggeration to say that there was something
ideal about her. She made the same impression on persons who only saw her
for an instant behind the grating, or who
knew her slightly in the convent. They
always felt for her instinctively the sympathy and respect inspired by the chosen few.
Religion may have rendered her humble ;
but nature made her modest, and endowed
her with all the virtues, charms, and noble
qualities that her enlightened conception
of Christianity only served to develop and
strengthen. In coming in contact with her,
one felt that there was no inward struggle in
her life, and that she naturally tended to all
that was good and beautiful. Everything
about her was harmonious; her figure was
grace and majesty combined, under her robe
and wimple. Her hands were lovely, — with
tapering, rounded fingers, finely formed, in
spite of a slight rheumatic stiffness of the
joints, that was not always perceptible. Her
voice was musical, and her enunciation exquisitely modulated and distinct, in English
as well as in French, — for she spoke both
languages perfectly. Born in France, of a

French mother and English father, she united the finest qualities of the two races, that seemed to constitute in her a perfect being. She had the dignified bearing, without the stiffness, of an Englishwoman, and there was no tinge of harshness in her religious austerity. When she reproved us, in a few well-chosen, simple words, we felt convicted. Her reproaches sank into our hearts, but were always accompanied by such hopeful encouragement, that we were humbled and subdued, without being in the least hurt, offended, or humiliated. We respected her for her sincerity, and loved her all the more because, with the sense of being unworthy of her friendship, there dawned the hope of some day deserving it; and this hope tended to become its own fulfilment.

Some of the nuns had daughters — one or more at a time — among the pupils; that is to say, at the request of the parents, or the child herself, with the permission of the Superior, there was a sort of maternal oversight. This adoption consisted in attention to physical or spiritual welfare, and in administering encouragement, or tender or severe rebuke, as the case might require.

The daughters were allowed to go to their mother's cell, to ask her advice and protection if needed, to take tea with her sometimes in the nuns' workroom, to give her some little present made by themselves, on her birthday, — to love her, in short, and to tell her that they loved her. Many aspired to be the daughter of Poulette or Mother Alippe. Madame Marie Xavier had several children; and not a few were very anxious to be adopted by Madame Alicia. But she was chary of such a favor. As secretary of the community, with all the Superior's office work to attend to, she had little leisure, and was often very tired. She had cherished one beloved daughter, — Louise de Courteilles, — who had gone away, and no one had dared to hope to fill her place; but I was audacious enough to entertain this idea, in my unsuspecting, childish simplicity. All the girls about me adored Madame Alicia, but did not venture to tell her of their devotion; but I went directly to her, without an idea of presumption.

"You?" said she, after hearing what I had to say, — "you, the naughtiest girl in the convent? Do you wish to make me do penance? What harm have I ever done you, to put it into your head to come to me and ask to be taken care of? Such an 'enfant terrible' as you, in the place of my good Louise, — that sweet, gentle child! You are either crazy, or else you bear me some grudge."

"Oh, no!" said I, without being at all disconcerted; "but won't you please to try? Who knows? — perhaps I may mend my ways, and become delightful just to please you."

"Ah," said she, "if that is it, — if it is with an idea of improving you that I must undertake this task, perhaps I may make up my mind to try the experiment; but as a means of saving my soul, I should have preferred some easier way."

"But an angel like Louise could not help save your soul," I argued. "There was no merit in taking care of her, and there will be a great deal in taking care of me."

"But suppose that with all the pains I take, I do not succeed in making you good and pious, — what then? Will you faithfully promise to help me yourself all you can?"

"I can't say," I answered. "I do not know yet what I really am, or what I want to be. I only know that I love you dearly; and I rather think that, whether I am good or bad, you will love me too."

"I see, Aurora, that you have a very good opinion of yourself."

"Oh, no; but I do need a mother. Be mine, in your own way; I am sure that you will do me good. You see I ask you to do it in my own interest, without any pretence. Come, dear mother, say 'Yes.' I warn you that I have already asked permission of my grandmother and the Superior, and that both of them mean to speak to you about it."

Madame Alicia then consented, and my astonished companions exclaimed, when I told them: "You are fortunate! You are just as bad as you can be; you are always in some mischief or other; and yet Madame Eugénie takes you under her wing, and now Madame Alicia loves you. What luck!"

"Yes, that is so," I answered, with the nonchalant fatuity of a careless child.

My affection, however, for this admirable woman, struck deeper roots than either of

us knew.   In spite of what seemed my
careless idleness, I had times of revery, and
even of discontented reflection, — which,
however, I kept to myself. Sometimes I was
so depressed, while committing the wildest
extravagances, that I was forced to say I
was in pain, to keep from breaking down.
My English companions would laugh, and
say, " How low-spirited you are to-day ! "
and when I was dejected, — in " a green
and yellow melancholy," — Isabella would
exclaim, " She is in the dumps, the absent-
minded creature ! " and then she would
make such a caricature of me that I could
not help laughing.   Nevertheless I kept
my own secret.   Certainly, if I had had
more strength of will, more initiative, I
should not have been a " diable " so long.
If any of the others had proposed to give
up our misdemeanors, I should have acceded
at once ; but I loved them, and they made
me laugh, and diverted me from my sad
thoughts.

Five minutes, though, with Madame Alicia did me a great deal more good ; because
in her severity I discerned — whether it
was friendship or Christian charity — a real
interest that made me happier with her

than I was with my young companions.
If I could have divided my time between
the work-room and my dear mother's cell,
in three days I should have been at a loss
to understand what amusement there could
be in climbing over roofs or exploring dark
cellars. I had needed to love and vener-
ate some one superior to myself, and I had
found such a person in Madame Alicia.
She was my ideal, — my holy mother.

When I had been a " diable " all day, I
would slip into my mother's cell at evening
after prayers. That was one of my privi-
leges as an adopted child. Prayers were
over at half-past eight. We went upstairs to
the dormitory, and saw in the long corridors
the nuns marching two by two on their
way to their cells, chanting Latin prayers
as they went along. Stopping before a
figure of the Virgin on the upper landing,
after several verses and responses they separated for the night, and each one entered
her cell without speaking ; for between
prayers and sleep, silence was imposed.
They, however, who were in attendance on
the sick, or who had adopted daughters,
were not subject to this regulation ; and I
had a right to go and see my mother for a

quarter of an hour between a quarter to
nine and nine o'clock. When the great
clock struck nine, her light must be put out,
and I must go back to my dormitory : so
that I only had five or six minutes sometimes, and even those were divided between
me and attention to the demi-semi-quarters
of the old clock ; for Madame Alicia was too
scrupulous to infringe upon the regulation,
even for a second.

"Well," she would say, opening her door,
at which I scratched to be let in, "so here
comes my torment!" That was what she
always called me; but her tone was so
sweet and cordial, her smile so tender, and
her expression so friendly, that I knew I
was welcome.

"Well, what news have you to tell me?
Have you been good to-day by accident?
No! but I see no night-cap." (That penal
head-dress had become almost chronic.)

"I have only worn it two hours this
evening."

"Ah! that is very well; and how was it
this morning?"

"I had it on in church, and I got behind the others so that you should not
see me."

"You need not do that; I hardly ever look at you, for fear of seeing that odious night-cap: and you will probably have it on again to-morrow?"

" Yes, I suppose so."

" Don't you mean ever to improve?"

" I can't yet."

" Then what do you come here for?"

" To see you, and to be scolded."

" That amuses you, then?"

" No; it does me good."

" I do not see that it does you the least good, and it does me harm; it troubles me, you naughty child!"

"So much the better!" I exclaimed. " That shows that you love me."

" And that *you* do not love *me*," she rejoined.

Then she gave me a good scolding. I liked to hear her, and listened with the greatest attention, as if I had resolved at last to amend my ways; but I had no definite plan of doing so.

" Come," said she, "you are going to act differently, I hope. You must be tired of this foolish behavior. Listen to the voice of God in your soul."

" Do you often pray to God for me?"

"Yes, often."

"Every day?"

"Yes, every day."

"Now you see, madame, that if I were good, you would not love me so much; I should be less in your thoughts."

She could not help laughing at this; for she had all the natural gayety inseparable from a heart at rest and a quiet conscience. Then she would take me by the shoulders and give me a good shaking, — as if to shake the Evil One out of me, — and put me out of the door just as the clock struck nine, laughing merrily. I would go up to the dormitory lighter-hearted, carrying with me the subtile influence of the serenity and frankness of her beautiful soul. But I shall have more to say of my dear Madame Alicia.

VIII.

THERE were four lay sisters in the convent, but I only remember two distinctly, — Sister Theresa and Sister Helen.

The former — who had christened me " Madcap" — was a tall old woman of an excellent type. Gay, rough, but kindness itself, she liked to laugh at us. She was a strong, active, raw-boned Scotchwoman, — sending us away often in a manner that showed she wanted us to come back, — amused with the tricks we played, but using her broomstick freely upon occasion. She liked " les diables," was not a bit afraid of them, and laughed louder than any one at our pranks.

Sister Theresa knew how to distil the mint-water for which our convent was famous. The mint was cultivated in great quantities in the nuns' garden. Three or four times a year it was mown, and heaped in a great cellar used as a laboratory.

This cellar was directly under our large schoolroom, and a wide staircase led to it, so that it was naturally one of our first halts when we started on an expedition; but when Sister Theresa was away the laboratory was carefully locked up, and when she was there we could not caper about among all her retorts and alembics. At such times we would stand at the open door and try to tease her; but she never seemed to mind.

However, by persistent efforts, I succeeded at last in getting a foothold in the sanctuary. For a long time I had only reconnoitred, but now I enjoyed watching her. All alone in the vast cellar, a strong light falling from above on her violet dress, coarse black veil, and strongly-marked, weather-beaten face, — she looked like one of Macbeth's witches stooping over the fire. Then again she would sit as still as a statue, close to the alembic, watching the precious fluid as it distilled drop by drop; or she would read the Bible to herself, and repeat her prayers in a hoarse, monotonous voice, — as beautiful in her old age as a portrait by Rembrandt.

One day when Sister Theresa was ab-

sorbed in her work, or fast asleep, I stole in
on tip-toe; and she did not know I was
there, till I was standing triumphant in the
midst of her fragile apparatus. Then she
was obliged to capitulate and satisfy my
curiosity. From that time she took a
fancy to me, and often let me come in. She
found that I was not clumsy, and would
not break anything ; moreover, she seemed
amused with my lounging about, and though
she often said that I ought to go back to
the schoolroom, she never put me out by
force, as she did some of the others. The
smell of the mint gave her a headache, and
its emanations hurt her eyes ; therefore she
liked to have me help her to spread and turn
her fragrant harvest; and on summer days,
when the heat became suffocating in the
schoolroom, I delighted in taking refuge
in this cool cellar, where the strong perfume
revived me.

The other lay sister— Sister Helen — was
the maid-of-all-work of the convent, making
the beds, sweeping the church, etc. She
became afterwards more dear to me than
any one save Madame Alicia ; but I was a
long time without noticing her. The two
other lay sisters did the cooking. Thus

there was an aristocracy and a democracy in the convent, as in the world. The choir sisters lived like patricians; their robes were white, and they wore fine linen, while the lay sisters worked hard, and their dark clothing was of a much coarser kind. They were women from the lower orders, uneducated; and they were unavoidably much less absorbed in ritual and devotions than in the household occupations of this great establishment. There were too few of them, however, to do all the work, and it became necessary to reinforce them by lay servants.

Upon the whole, it was a genial family of women. I do not remember one disagreeable girl; and with the exception of my experience with Miss D——, I met with nothing but kindness and forbearance from nuns and teachers. It is impossible not to cherish the memory of the most tranquil, if not the happiest years of my life. Of course there was physical as well as moral suffering; but never, before nor since, have I had so little reason to complain of others.

IX.

MY first grief after I entered the upper class was the departure of Isabella, whose parents took her away to travel in Switzerland. She left us, delighted at the prospect of such a journey, — regretting no one, apparently, but Sophia, and paying very little attention to my woe. That hurt my feelings. I loved Sophia too, and was doubly jealous, — in the first place, because she preferred Isabella to me; and then because Isabella liked her better. For some days I was in great affliction; but when I saw how much Sophia missed her friend, I begged her to let me sympathize with her sorrow. Though she seemed at first to care little for my efforts at consolation, I entreated her very humbly to be as miserable as she liked when she was with me, and to talk of Isabella to her heart's content, without fearing to weary my patience and affection. Then Sophia exclaimed, throwing her arms around my neck, —

"I wonder why Isabella and I have always treated you as if you were a little
child! You have so much feeling! and I
want you to be my real friend; only you
must always let me love Isabella the best.
She comes first; but after her, I am sure I
love you better than any one else here."

I joyfully accepted the second place, and
became from this moment Sophia's inseparable companion. She was always lovely
and engaging, but I must acknowledge
that I was the more devoted and enthusiastic of the two; for, exclusive by nature,
she could not well divide her affection.
Sometimes I accused her of ingratitude;
then I felt that I was wrong; and without
neglecting her, opened my heart to other
friendships.

Mary had gone to England to stay a
short time. My grief was not very great.
because I had seen very little of her since
I left the lower class, and I thought that
on her return she would be promoted also;
but after a prolonged absence, she came
back to the lower division.

A new friendship now absorbed and
consoled me; for I found Fanelly de
Brissac the most loving of all my school

companions. She was a little blonde, as
fresh as a rose, — with such an animated,
frank, kind face, that it did one good to
look at her. Her beautiful light hair fell in
curls over her blue eyes and plump cheeks ;
and as she was always in motion, running
when most girls walked, and bounding
like a ball when others ran, the perpetual
undulation of her golden tresses was a delight to the eyes. Her red lips were always parted with a smile ; and, being a
native of Nérac, she spoke French with
the most bewitching little Gascon accent.
Her horizontal eyebrows almost met above
her nose, and her radiant eyes sparkled
like stars. She was always doing or plan-
ning something, chattering all the time,
and constantly on the wing like a butterfly.
Ardent, loving, sunny-tempered, she was a
perfect southern type, — the sweetest and
most engaging companion I ever had. She
loved me first, and told me so frankly, without waiting to see how I would receive her
advances ; but I responded at once heartily,
without stopping to think. My good star
evidently presided over this impulse, for I
found in her a perfect treasure of sweetness, — the gentleness of an angel with the

vivacity of a sprite. She possessed such buoyancy of physical and moral health, such inexhaustible kindness, such eager, active, ingenious endeavors to make people happy about her, such unfailing and instinctive generosity, as made a rare union of qualities, — a character perfectly reliable, without a single flaw. Any one seeing her so gay and volatile, with her hair all flying about her face, might have supposed she was thoughtless; while in reality she was always thinking of others, living in the affection she had for them and the hope of contributing to their pleasure. I can see her now entering the schoolroom (she was constantly going in and out), peering right and left to find me, — for in spite of her beautiful eyes she was near-sighted.

"Where is my aunt?" she would say (the name by which she called me). "What have you done with my aunt? Young ladies, young ladies, who has seen my aunt?"

"Here I am," I would say. "Come and sit by me."

"That is right; you have kept my place. Good! now we shall have a fine time.

What is the matter, auntie? You look troubled. Tell me what is the matter. Nothing? Well, then, laugh. Are you getting tired? Yes, that is so. Come, let us go off; I have found something delightful."

And she would take me to the garden or the cloisters in search of amusement; or perhaps she had prepared some surprise. In her society it was not possible to be sad or dreamy; and, strange to say, her perpetual motion was never wearisome. She took possession of her companion, and one never regretted yielding to her charm. For me she was health and strength, for body and soul.

We had in the convent a childish notion of respecting the priority of friendship, and we exacted it of one another. We used to make out a list of our intimates in regular succession; and the initials of the four or five favorite names decorated, like heraldic devices, the walls, our copy-books, and the tops of our desks. When the first place had been once taken, we had no right to give it to another; priority was an obligation. Thus my list, while I was in the upper class, always consisted of Isabella Clifford at the head; then came

Sophia Cary; Fanelly could only have the third place, although I loved her more than the others, and she had no friend but me. She accepted, however, without pain or jealousy, this inferior rank. After her came Anna Vié, who took the fourth place; and for a year I had no other intimacies. The name of Madame Alicia, however, crowned the list; and she was placed above them all, alone. The initials of my four companions formed the word "ISFA," which I wrote on everything that belonged to me, like a cabalistic formula. Sometimes it was surrounded by a halo of little *a's*, to show that Alicia filled all the rest of my heart. How often Madame Eugénie, — who, even with her poor eyes, saw everything, — in examining our papers, puzzled herself over this mysterious word! Since we all had a logogriph of some kind, she was inclined to think it must be a sort of cipher, in which we were conspiring against her authority; but when she questioned us, we all said that it was a word we used to try our pens Mystery is so delightful, — especially when the secret is transparent!

Anna Vié, my fourth letter, was very intelligent, gay, fond of mischief and ridicule,

— the wittiest girl in school and the most amusing. Poor, and unprepossessing in appearance, we loved her all the more for these two disadvantages, of which she was always making fun herself. She was an orphan, under the care of an old Greek uncle, whom she hardly knew, and of whom she was very much afraid. A leader among "les diables," very high-tempered, and dreaded on account of her sharp tongue, she had, nevertheless, a noble, generous heart. Her sparkling gayety masked a great deal of real bitterness ; but the future that she dreaded, her wit that made her more feared than loved by most of the girls, her poor little shabby black gowns, her small undeveloped figure, her yellow, bilious complexion, her queer little eyes, all were for her subjects of constant jest and ceaseless pain. Some said she was envious of others' advantages; but it was not so. She had excellent good sense; there was no meanness about her; and when she became intimate enough with us not to laugh at us or with us all the time, she excited our sympathy by her reticent unhappiness. We talked a great deal about a favorite project of mine, — of taking her to Nohant to live. My grandmother consented, but Anna's uncle vetoed the plan.

For nearly a year, Sophia, Fanelly, Anna, and I were inseparable. I was the connecting link ; for till Sophia accepted me for her second friend, and the two others had given me the first place, they had had little to do with one another. Our intimacy was unclouded, though it pained me sometimes that Sophia felt herself obliged to love the absent Isabella more than me ; and then I thought it my bounden duty to love the absent Isabella and indifferent Sophia more than Fanelly and Anna, who adored me without any reserve. But that was the rule, the law ; if we had disturbed the order of the list, we should have thought ourselves guilty of the most reprehensible fickleness. However, I must say that in spite of all, I knew that I loved Fanelly more than all the others ; and I often told her, very illogically, that by my will she was the third on the list, but that against my will she was my best, perhaps my only real, friend. Then she would answer, laughingly, " What difference does that make, whether I am the third or not, so long as you love me as much as I love you ? That is all I ask of my aunt. I am not too proud to love all the girls you are fond of."

After some months Isabella came back from Switzerland, but only to say good-by; she was now to live in England. I was in great affliction, — all the more because, engrossed by Sophia, who absorbed all her attention, she hardly took any notice of me, except to turn round and say, "What makes that child cry so?" That was the "unkindest cut of all;" but when Sophia told her that I had been her comforter, and that she had adopted me as her second friend, Isabella condescended to console me, and even invited me to join them in their walk. She made one more appearance among us, and then went away. I heard that she married a very wealthy man, but I never saw her again.

A year, indeed nearly eighteen months, slipped by almost unconsciously, and I was still a "diable." Sophia and Anna often declared that they were tired to death of the convent; and whether because it was the fashion, or because they were really sick of this life, all my companions said the same thing. Those who were devout thought it wrong to complain; but they did not seem happy.

Most of these children probably regretted pleasant homes; and those who had none — Anna Vié, for instance — did nothing but dream of balls and parties, of travelling, of all sorts of delights consistent with freedom and incompatible with regular, serious occupation. Seclusion and the monotony of a studious life seem in fact to ·be particularly distasteful to young girls.

I was happier, however, in the convent than anywhere else: no one there was sufficiently well acquainted with my past life to talk of what I must expect in the future; and that is what one's relatives always have in view. It is their tender care, their constant preoccupation. They try to make your future secure; and then somehow fate foils all their plans. Moreover, children seldom profit by their parents' advice; their instinctive independence and curiosity constantly excite them to opposition. Nuns have not the same kind of solicitude for the children under their care; they think of nothing but heaven and hell, and for them the girl's future is her soul's salvation.

Even before my conversion, this spiritual future had no terrors for me. Since, according to the Catholic religion, one can choose between salvation and perdition; since grace abounds, and our own free will may set our feet in the path where the angels themselves deign to guide us, I used to say to myself in my vainglorious self-reliance that I should attend to that one of these days; but I was in no haste to do so. I had never worried a great deal about myself, — certainly not in matters of religion. I wanted to love God for the sake of loving him; I did not want to be afraid of him, and I always said so when others tried to frighten me.

Thus thoughtlessly, without anxiety about this life or the one to come, I let the days slip by, only thinking of my own amusement, — or rather not thinking about anything at all, — always ready to go in search of pleasure with my friends. Anna liked to talk to me, and I loved to listen to her. Sophia was dreamy and sad; I followed her about silently, not disturbing her meditations, and never upbraiding her when she shook off her lethargy. Fanelly loved excitement, was always gay, ferreting about or setting on foot some mischief or other. With her I was full of fun, ardor, and motion.

Fortunately, she liked to take the lead. Anna followed us from affection, and Sophia because she had nothing else to do; thus we spent whole days deep in mischief. Sometimes we planned to meet in an out-of-the-way place, where Fanelly, who had more money than either of us, and who knew besides how to cajole the old porter into buying everything she wanted, had prepared some delightful surprise, generally something good to eat, — magnificent melons, cakes, baskets of cherries or grapes, fritters, *pâtés*, — all sorts of things; she was marvellously ingenious in regaling us with the most unexpected dainties.

For a whole summer we almost lived on the fruit of this smuggling. What a diet! Any one over fifteen would have had a fit of sickness in consequence. I contributed to these " treats " the dainties given me by Mother Alicia and also by Sister Theresa, who used to make in her laboratory the most delicious things, with which she stuffed my pockets. To share these treasures, and feast secretly between meals, against the rules, was a delight, a high festival, — and we indulged in fits of laughter over rather vulgar pranks, such as tossing up to the ceiling the bottom of a pie filled with sweetmeats, and seeing it stick; hiding chicken bones in a piano, or dropping fruit-parings on dark staircases so as to make solemn persons slip. All that seemed to us very witty, intoxicated as we were with our own merriment, and with nothing else, — for we never had anything to drink on these occasions but water and lemonade. The search for the victim was kept up, checked from time to time by some great disappointment.

X.

SO far as studies were concerned, I did nothing but learn a little — a very little — Italian, music, and drawing. I readily applied myself to nothing but English; and I did this because one lost half the pleasure of life in the convent, if one did not understand that language.

I also began to want to write. It was the fashion; those who had no inspiration wrote letters to one another, often charming in their tenderness and simplicity. This correspondence was contrary to the rules; but that only made it more interesting. That, and other severe restrictions — prohibition of kisses, insisting that there should always be three instead of two together — seemed to me a great error in the system of convent education. Most of us, however, brought up in our own families, attributed these rules to a desire to restrain human affection, which should be devoted exclusively to the Creator.

I began of course by writing verses, rebelling against the Alexandrine, which I understood, however, perfectly. I tried to preserve a sort of rhythm without attending to the rhyme or the cæsura, and composed many verses that had a great success among the girls, who were not very critical. At last I took it into my head to write a novel; and though I was not at all religious at that time, I made my story very pious and edifying. It was more of a tale, however, than a novel. The hero and heroine met in the dusk of evening, in the country, at the foot of a shrine, where they had come to say their prayers. They admired and exhorted each other by turns. I knew that they ought to fall in love, but I could not manage it. Sophia urged me on; but when I had described them both as beautiful and perfect beings, when I had brought them together in an enchanting spot at the entrance of a Gothic chapel under the shade of lofty oaks, I never could get any further. It was not possible for me to describe the emotions of love; I had not a word to say, and gave it up. I succeeded in making them ardently pious, — not that I knew any more about piety than I did about love;

but I had examples of piety all the time before my eyes, and perhaps even then the germ was unconsciously developing within me. At all events, my young couple, after several chapters of travel and adventure that I have completely forgotten, separated at last, both consecrating themselves to God, — the heroine taking the veil, and the hero becoming a priest.

Sophia and Anna thought my novel very well written, and they liked some things about it; but they declared that the hero (who rejoiced, by the way, in the name of Fitzgerald) was dreadfully tiresome, and they did not seem to consider the heroine much more amusing. There was a mother whom they liked better; but upon the whole my prose was less successful than my verses, and I was not much charmed with it myself.

Then I wrote a pastoral romance in verse, still worse than the novel; and one winter day I put it into the stove. Then I stopped writing, and decided that it was not an amusing occupation, though I had taken infinite delight in the preliminary composition.

In the middle of my second year in the

convent my grandmother came back to Paris, and I was allowed to go out several times. She did not think me improved in appearance or manners, and said that I was more absent-minded than ever. The dancing-lessons of M. Abraham — a former teacher of Marie Antoinette — had not made me graceful, though he had done his best. He used to come in court dress, black silk stockings, and knee-breeches, with buckled shoes, a powdered wig with a queue, a diamond ring on his finger, and a violin in his hand. He was about eighty, but had a slender, graceful, even elegant figure, delicate features, and a pleasant, wrinkled face, all veined in red and blue on a yellow background, like an autumn leaf. He was an excellent man, polite, solemn, distinguished, the very pink of propriety. He gave his lessons in the Superior's large parlor, to about fifteen girls at a time; and on this occasion we were all outside the grating.

After some geometrical illustrations of grace, and drill in the customary dancing-steps, he would seat himself in an arm-chair, and say: "Now, young ladies, I am the King or Queen, as the case may be; and as you will all doubtless be presented at court,

8

let us practise the way of entering the room, and also of retiring after the presentation, with the appropriate courtesies." At other times we practised less thrilling solemnities, imagining a drawing-room filled with guests. He made some of us sit down, while others entered or took their leave; and he taught us how to speak to the mistress of the house, then to a princess, duchess, marchioness, countess, viscountess, baroness, and lady presiding, each with the measure of respect due to her rank. Then he took by turns the part of a prince, duke, marquis, etc., and came to speak to us in that character, so that we might learn to respond properly. We had to put on and take off our gloves, use a fan, smile, get up and sit down, cross the room, — in short do everything imaginable. It seemed as if in this antiquated French politeness everything must be done by rule, — even sneezing.

We were all ready to burst out laughing, and made no end of intentional mistakes to exasperate him; but toward the end of the lesson, so as to send the excellent old man away happy, we pretended to have learned something, and put on all the airs and graces we could muster to please him. It would have been too cruel to go on vexing such a kind and patient teacher. But it was very hard to follow his directions with proper gravity, though in this way we learned how to act. Certainly old-fashioned grace must have been very different from what goes by that name nowadays; for the more absurd and affected we were, the more he praised us.

In spite of all M. Abraham's lessons, I was still round-shouldered, with abrupt, unconventional manners and an utter abhorrence of gloves and low courtesies. My grandmother scolded me a great deal for these shortcomings. The days when I was allowed to leave the convent were mainly occupied with visits to some of her old countesses, to whom she wished to introduce me, apparently with the hope of interesting them in me, and laying the foundation of future social relations; but most of these ladies seemed to me very uncongenial. In the evening we dined at my uncle's, or with my cousins, and it was always time to go back to the convent just when I began to feel somewhat at ease. In the morning I would start joyous and alert, and reach my grandmother's full of impatient expectation; but after two or three hours a chill would come over me, — particularly as the moment of departure drew near, — and I was never calm and gay till I found myself back again in the convent.

XI.

THE pleasantest thing that happened to me about this time was having a cell to myself. Each of the young ladies of the upper class had one, but I had been kept in the dormitory on account of my unruly ways. In this dormitory under the roof it was suffocating in summer, and freezing in winter; and one could hardly ever pass a night undisturbed, for there was always some child who cried out with pain or terror. And then, never to be in one's own room, never to be alone by day or by night, is very hard for those who like to think and dream. Life in common is ideal when people are fond of one another; I have realized this in the convent, and I shall never forget it: but every thoughtful person needs times of solitude and reflection, for in this way only one can enjoy thoroughly the sweetness of companionship.

The cell that they gave me was the worst in the convent, — a garret room at the farthest end of the building, adjoining the church. The next, similar to mine, was occupied by Coralie le Narrois, a very austere, but simple, pious, timid creature, whose proximity it was thought would inspire me with awe.

However, we got along very well together, in spite of the difference in our tastes ; for I took great care not to disturb her sleep or devotions when I slipped out noiselessly to meet Fanelly and other light-minded comrades on the staircase : and then we would wander about till late at night in the organ-loft perhaps, or in the garret where they kept onions. We had to pass close to the door of Maria Josepha, one of the servants ; but she was always a sound sleeper.

My cell was about ten feet long by six wide, and so low that, lying in bed, my head touched the sloping roof. The door, when it opened, grazed the bureau close to the window opposite ; and I could not shut it without getting into the embrasure of this window, consisting of four panes, looking on a projecting gutter that completely hid from view the court below. But the outlook was superb ; I saw

a part of Paris over the tops of our great
horse-chestnut trees, and large nurseries
and kitchen gardens spread out below,
encircling our domain. But for the sil-
houettes of houses and public buildings
against the sky, I might have fancied myself, if not in the country, at least in an
immense village. The bell-tower of the
convent and the low cloisters stood out
in the foreground; and by night, especially by moonlight, the effect was very
picturesque.

I heard the clock strike close by; and
though at first that prevented me from
sleeping, I became gradually accustomed to
its ponderous, melancholy chime, and liked
to lie there, half asleep and half awake,
listening to the far-away nightingales taking up again their interrupted song.

My furniture consisted of a wooden
painted bedstead, an old bureau, a straw-
bottomed chair, a miserable little rug, and
a small Louis XV. harp, extremely pretty,
which had gleamed under the white arms of
my grandmother in her youthful days, and
on which I was learning to accompany myself when I sang. For this purpose I was
allowed to practise in my cell; and this

became an excuse for passing an hour there every day alone. In truth, I rarely practised at all; but this hour of solitude and revery became very precious. The sparrows hopped in boldly, and ate even on my bed the crumbs I gave them. Although this poor little cell was an oven in summer, and in winter literally an ice-house, — the moisture from the roof congealing and forming stalactites in the cracks of my dilapidated ceiling, — I was so much attached to the place that I remember kissing the walls fondly when I left. A whole world of dreams and experience seemed to abide in this little dusty, miserable nook. There alone I was myself, belonged to myself alone. By day I thought of nothing in particular; I watched the clouds, the branches of the trees, the swallows' flight. By night I lay and listened to the distant, confused murmur of the great city, that died away and was lost in the rural sounds of our suburb. As soon as the day dawned, the noises of the convent began, and drowned the outside clamor. Our cocks crowed, the bells rang for matins, and the blackbirds in the garden repeated over and over again their morning song. The monotonous voices of

the nuns chanting the service came faintly
to my ears, penetrating every fissure of the
sonorous pile. The hoarse cries of the
venders of provisions rose from the court
below, contrasting with the cadences of
the nuns' sweet chant; and finally the
shrill call of Maria Josepha came nearer
and nearer as she hurried from room to
room, and pushing back the creaking bolts
of the doors that closed the passages, put
an end to my listening.

The studies for which my grandmother
gave up the pleasure of having me at
home amounted to nothing. She laid
great stress upon accomplishments; and
as a " diable " emeritus, I took no interest
in my lessons. In truth, I was getting
sick of this aimless waste of time; but it
had become a habit difficult to break.

XII.

THERE came all at once, however, a great change in my life; and a passionate devotion blazed up spontaneously in a soul ignorant of itself. I was weary of idleness, of yielding to the caprices of my companions or following their lead, — tired, in short, of our long-continued, systematic rebellion against discipline. My worshipful love for Madame Alicia was a calm affection, and I needed some ardent passion. I was fifteen years old, with a great yearning for love, and a void in my heart. Personal vanity was not yet aroused, and I felt none of the inordinate solicitude about my own appearance so common in almost all the young girls of my age. I needed to love some one or some thing that was not myself; and I knew no one on earth whom I could love with all my might. I did not turn to God; but what Christians call divine grace came down to me, and took possession of me as if by surprise. I had

listened with indifference to the exhorta-
tions of the nuns; even Madame Alicia
herself had not influenced me consciously.
This is the way it happened. I shall simply relate the facts, without attempting any
explanation; for there is a mystery in these
processes, these sudden transformations of
our innermost souls, which it is not well
to try to unveil, even to ourselves.

We went to mass at seven every morning,
as I have said; and at four in the afternoon we returned to the church for half an
hour, — which was passed by the devoutly
inclined in prayer, meditation, or some religious reading. The others yawned, took
naps, or whispered when the teacher was
not watching them. One day, for want of
occupation, I opened a book that had been
given into my hands, and which I had not
yet thought of reading. The leaves were
still stuck together by the coloring on
the edges. It was an abridgment of the
" Lives of the Saints; " and glancing at
the pages, my eye was caught by the
strange legend of Saint Simeon Stylites, so
ridiculed by Voltaire. In fact, it is much
more the story of an Indian fakir than
of a Christian philosopher. The legend

first made me smile; then its originality
captivated me. I read it over again with
interest, and thought it even more poetical
than absurd. The next day I read another
story, and on the following devoured several with avidity. I did not care for the
miracles related; but the faith, the courage,
the endurance of these martyrs seemed to
me glorious, and made some hidden chord
vibrate in my soul.

There was at the back of the choir a
superb picture by Titian, that I could
never see distinctly. Very dark itself,
and hung too high in a corner where
there was little light, it was hard to distinguish anything more than masses of rich
color on a sombre background. The subject was Jesus in the Garden of Olives.
He was represented fainting in the arms of
an attendant angel. The kneeling Saviour
had sunk down, one of his arms sustained
by those of the angel, who supported on
his breast that beautiful, ghastly, agonized
head. I sat opposite this picture, and
had looked at it so constantly that at last
I divined, more than comprehended, its
meaning. There was one time only when
I could see the details clearly. This was

in winter, when the rays of the setting sun fell on the red drapery of the angel and the white, bare arm of the Christ. The glitter of the glass gave it for a few moments a transcendent beauty; and at that instant I always felt a thrill of emotion, even when I was far from being devout, and never dreamed that I could become so.

As I turned over the pages of the "Lives of the Saints," my eyes wandered continually to this picture. It was in summer; the setting sun no longer illumined the painting, but the contemplated object was visible to my mind, if not to my eyes. Looking fixedly at those great masses of color, I sought the hidden meaning of such a keen, voluntary sorrow, and began to apprehend something far deeper and grander than anything I had ever been told. I grew very sad myself, as if in sympathy, — deeply distressed, and touched to the heart by pain and pity such as I had never before imagined. Unbidden tears rushed to my eyes; but I brushed them away, ashamed to be overcome by my feelings without knowing why. It could not have been the beauty of the picture; for it was so indistinct that I should only have said it looked as if it must be beautiful. There was another painting in the choir, that we could see better; but it was far less remarkable. It represented Saint Augustine under the fig-tree, with the miraculous sunbeam on which was written the famous " Tolle, lege," — the mysterious words that the son of Monica thought he heard in the branches, — a command that decided him to open and read the Gospels.

I found the Life of Saint Augustine, of which I knew something already; for the saint, as the patron of our order, was held in especial veneration in the convent. The story delighted me with its impress of sincerity and enthusiasm. Then I read the Life of Saint Paul, and the " Cur me persequeris ? " made a deep impression on me. The little Latin that I had learned at home enabled me to understand a part of the services. I began to listen, and to discover in the Psalms, recited every day by the nuns, admirable poetic simplicity. In short, for a whole week the Catholic religion seemed to me a very interesting study.

" Tolle, lege," decided me also, at last, to open the New Testament and read the Gospels over attentively. The first impression was not strong; there was no novelty in the Holy Book. I had always enjoyed the beauty of the narrations; but my grandmother had tried so hard to show me the absurdity of the miracles, and had repeated so many of Voltaire's witticisms, — especially what he says of the evil spirits escaping into the herd of swine, — that I had looked at it all very sceptically under her influence, and was not now particularly moved, even in reading of the agony and death of Jesus.

That day, at nightfall, I was sadly pacing the cloisters. All my friends were in the garden, and there were no teachers near. I was not at all in the mood for a frolic; in fact, I had come away to avoid my companions, — for I felt disgusted with the inanity of my life, and asked myself: "Is there any new thing left for a 'diable' to do, after all?" Some of the nuns passed, and a few boarders; they were going to pray or meditate in the church, each one separately, as was the pious custom at this hour of recreation.

The idea occurred to me to follow them, put some ink in the holy-water font, or tie

Whisky by one leg to the cloister bell-rope;
but these things had been done so many
times already that they were old tricks.
I saw plainly that I had exhausted the
resources of my disorderly career, and that
something new must be done. But what?
Even if I could, I did not want to be
one of the good girls, — most assuredly
not a stupid one; and I said to myself:
" To-day I have tried; I have read the
Holy Book, — the life and teachings of
the Redeemer, — and my heart was not
touched, and I do not believe it ever will
be."   Several devotees just then passed
along in the gloom, going by themselves
to pour out their contrite souls before a
God of love and forgiveness. I had a curiosity to see what they did, and how they
manifested their devotion in solitude, —
especially a humpbacked old woman, one
of the lodgers, who stole by looking more
like a witch than one of the wise virgins.
" I mean to go and see," I said to myself,
" how that little monster wriggles about on
her bench; when I tell the other ' diables,'
it will make them laugh."   I followed her,
crossed the chapter-house, and entered the
church.   We were not allowed to go there

at this time of the evening without a special permission ; and this was another inducement, — for I felt that it was not derogatory to a " diable " to smuggle herself in. It is singular that the first time I ever entered a church of my own accord it was against the rules, and with the intention of committing a shameful action.

Hardly had I set foot in the church than I entirely forgot my old woman, who trotted along and disappeared in some nook as if she had been a rat. She vanished also from my thoughts, I was so charmed and impressed with the aspect of the church itself by night. It was really more a chapel than a church, and had nothing remarkable about it except its exquisite neatness. An oblong building, with freshly whitewashed walls and no architectural pretension whatever, it was more like a Protestant conventicle than a Catholic place of worship. There were, as I have said, a few pictures in the choir; on the simple altar, decked with pretty silken stuffs, stood massive silver candlesticks, and beautiful flowers constantly renewed. The nave was divided into three parts, — one intended for the use of priests and privileged guests on festival days ; the front choir for

9

the pupils, servants, and residents; and last, the chancel, appropriated to the nuns. This part of the sanctuary had an inlaid floor, waxed every morning and carefully polished; and here also were the nuns' stalls, arranged in a semicircle against the wall. They were of walnut, and shone like glass. A high grating with very small interstices, and a grated iron door never closed, made a line of separation between the sisters and ourselves. On each side of this door heavy fluted rococo wooden pillars supported the organ, as well as an open gallery thrown across like a "jubé" between the two parts of the church. Thus, contrary to custom, the organ stood out almost in the centre of the nave, and added greatly to the effect of our voices when we sang motets and choruses on great occasions. The part of the choir reserved for the pupils was paved with sepulchral slabs; and on the old flagstones were inscribed epitaphs of prioresses who had died before the Revolution, with names of ecclesiastics, and even of laymen, of the time of James Stuart. I remember the name of Throckmorton under our feet; and it was said that if you went into the church at midnight, all these

dead men pushed up the stones with their
fleshless skulls and glared at you, beseech-
ing your prayers.

In spite of these associations, and the
obscurity of the church, the impression I received that night was not gloomy. There
was no light save that which came from
the little silver lamp in the chancel, and its
white flame was imaged in the polished
floor like a star in a pool of water. This
reflected light touched here and there the
fretted picture frames, gleamed on the chis-
elled candlesticks, and glimmered on the
gilded sheathing of the tabernacle. The
door at the back of the chancel was wide
open on account of the heat, as well as
one of the large windows above the burial-
ground. The perfume of jessamine and
honeysuckle was borne to me on the wings
of a refreshing breeze. A star, lost in
immensity, framed by the open window,
seemed to look at me intently. Nightingales were singing in the distance. I had
never felt before the charm and mystery of
this holy peace, and I gave myself up to the
new delight. By and by the few persons
scattered about the church went out noiselessly. A nun who had been kneeling in

the chancel, wishing apparently to read after her meditation, came forward to light her taper at the lamp swinging before the altar. The sisters did not merely bend the knee, but prostrated themselves literally, as if bowed to the earth before the Holy of Holies. This nun was tall and stately: it must have been Madame Eugénie, Madame Marie Xavier, or Madame Monica; but we never could recognize these ladies in church, for their faces were covered by their veils, and they wore long black woollen mantles that disguised the figure and swept the floor. The sombre dress; the slow, noiseless motions; the simple, graceful gesture with which she lifted her arm to grasp the ring and bring the shining silver lamp within her reach; the strong light thrown on her black form as she slid the cresset back to its place; her long, reverent prostration before the altar; the noiseless, graceful way in which she returned to her stall, even the impersonality of the unknown nun (who might have been, for aught I knew, a phantom from the past, on the point of disappearing beneath the storied slabs, to lie down again on her marble couch), — all filled me with emotions of mingled terror and delight.

Enraptured with the poetry of the place, I lingered long after the nun had finished reading and had gone away. It was growing late; prayers were over, and it was time to close the church. I had lost all sense of time. I do not know exactly how it was, but it seemed as if I were breathing an atmosphere of indescribable sweetness, inhaling it more with my soul than with my senses. All at once I felt something like a shock, and grew dizzy. A white light flashed before my eyes, in which I gradually seemed enveloped. I thought I heard a whisper in my ear, " Tolle, lege ! " I turned quickly round, thinking that Mother Alicia was speaking to me; but I was alone !

Knowing well that I was under a sort of hallucination, I was neither elated nor terrified. I did not say to myself that it was a miracle, or even a vainglorious deception, but I tried to see things as they really were; only I felt sure that faith had taken possession of my heart, — as I had always hoped it might, — and my face was bathed in tears of happiness and gratitude. I knew, too, that at last I loved God; that my thought unquestioning embraced that ideal justice, tenderness, and holiness, whose existence I had never doubted, but with which I had never been in direct communication. I felt all at once that this communication was established, — as if an insurmountable barrier had suddenly given way between the source of infinite life and the slumbering forces of my soul. I saw a long vista stretch out endlessly before me, and I longed to tread that road. There was no more doubt or lukewarmness, and it never even occurred to me that I could regret or ridicule this passionate excitement; for I was one of those who never look behind, — who hesitate a long time before passing the Rubicon, — but who, once on the other side, lose sight entirely of the shore they have just left. "Yes, the veil is lifted," I softly exclaimed! "I see the light, and I shall walk toward it. But, first of all, let me give thanks."

To whom, and how? I said to the unknown God who had drawn me to him. "What is thy name? How shall I pray? What words worthy of thee, and capable of expressing love, can my soul utter? I know not; but thou readest my thoughts, thou knowest that I love thee!"— and my tears broke forth at last like rain. I sobbed convulsively; I fell prostrate behind my bench, and literally watered the floor with my tears.

The sister who came in to close the church heard me weeping, and came to me in some alarm. I do not think she recognized me, and I did not know her under her veil in the darkness. Quickly rising, I passed by her without looking up or speaking, and groped my way back to my cell.

The prayers were all over; but I had prayed more fervently than any of the girls that night, and I soon fell asleep, overcome with fatigue, yet in a state of indescribable beatitude. The next day the Countess, who had happened to remark my absence from prayers, asked me where I had been all the evening. I had never been a liar, and now I answered promptly, "In the church." She looked at me for a moment in doubt, but saw that I was speaking the truth, and kept silence. I was not punished, but I do not know what she thought of my answer. Strange to say, I did not go at once to Madame Alicia and pour out my heart. I said nothing to my friends, "les diables;" for I felt reticent about my

new-found happiness, though not in the
least ashamed. What other people would
think did not much concern me, and I was
like a miser with the treasure of my joy. I
awaited impatiently the hour for meditation
in the church. The " Tolle, lege," of my
ecstatic vision was ringing in my ears, and
I longed to read again the sacred book;
yet I did not open it, but thought it all
over, — knowing it almost by heart. The
miraculous part, which had been such a
stumbling-block, troubled me no longer.
Not only did I feel no inclination to ex-
amine critically, but I despised the idea of
doing so. After the deep emotion I had
experienced, I said to myself that I should
be demented, and my own worst enemy,
coolly to try and analyze, comment upon,
or discuss the source of such ecstatic
delight.

At the end of four or five days, Anna,
remarking that I was silent and·absorbed,
and that I went to church every evening,
said, with astonishment, —

" My dear· 'note-book' [that was the
name she had given me], what does all this
mean? Can it be that you have actually
become pious? "

" I have become pious, my child," I answered quietly.

" That is impossible."

" I give you my word of honor that I am
speaking the truth."

" Well," she said, after thinking a minute, " I shall say nothing to dissuade you,
— in the first place, because I do not believe it would be of any use; and then I
have always said that you are an impulsive
creature. But you must not expect me to
follow your example; I am naturally scep-
tical, and reason about things. I envy you
your happiness, and think you are right
not to hesitate; but I do not believe that
I shall ever be satisfied without proof. If
such a miracle came to pass, however, I
should do the same, I acknowledge."

" Shall you love me less?" I asked.

" If I did, it would not afflict you now,"
she answered; "devotion is all-absorbing,
and makes up for everything. But I believe
you are perfectly sincere, and I shall remain
your friend just the same."

She went on to speak very affectionately, and never failed to be from that time
sensible, considerate, and even indulgent.

Sophia was not much affected by the

change that had been wrought in me. She had always been a sober sort of a " diable," having occasional fits of devotion and moments of depression that she could never explain and did not like to acknowledge. It was becoming rather unfashionable to be a " diable," and my conversion seemed to give the institution, its finishing stroke. Perhaps the others, like me, were secretly tired of so much dissipation.

Fanelly was the one whom I feared most to grieve ; but she spared me the pain of refusing to join her sports by coming to me at once and saying : " So, my aunt, you are going to be good ! Well, if that makes you happy, I am glad ; and if you like, I will be good too. I am willing to be pious, so as to do just what you do, and stay always with you."

If that had depended on an affectionate impulse, it would have been as she said ; but she was too unstable. In truth, among " les diables " Anna and I were the only ones susceptible of what is technically called conversion. The others were not pious, because they were too frivolous ; but they were not unbelievers, and the moment our misdemeanors came to an end, they became a little more regular in pious practices, without being a whit more fervent than before.

Anna was strong-minded. That word describes her perfectly, because she had a great deal of intellect and will; while I had neither strength of mind nor force of will. There was nothing strong in me but passion; and when that took the form of religion, it consumed my heart, and nothing in my intellect opposed it. Anna became pious after her marriage, but so long as she remained in the convent, she was steadfast in her unbelief.

I kept up my intimacy with Louise de la Rochejaquelein. She was still in the lower division, being one of the younger girls; but she was always more sensible and better informed than I was. I met her in the cloisters a few days after my change of heart; since she was neither good, stupid, nor a " diable," her judgment would be unbiassed, and I was curious to know what she would say.

" Well," she asked, " are you going on in the same way; are you just as much of a reprobate as ever?"

" What should you say," I answered, " if I told you that I had become very religious?"

" I should say that you were doing right, and I should love you more than ever."

She kissed me most affectionately, without attempting any encouragement to persevere, — perceiving, undoubtedly, how enthusiastic I was.

Mary came back about this time. She had grown a head taller; her expression was more boyish, and her manners even more impetuous and independent than formerly. She re-entered the lower class, and became so uproarious that her relatives took her away after a few months. She was never tired of laughing at my piety; and whenever we met she made me the butt of her unsparing ridicule. I was not angry, however; for she was so gay and free from malice that she made fun of me without hurting my feelings. We met long afterwards, when we were both upwards of forty, with unabated affection for each other, and hearty reciprocal enjoyment in talking over old times.

My sudden conversion hardly allowed me time to breathe. Absorbed as I was in this new passion, I was eager to taste all its delights, and made haste to see my confessor, that I might be officially reconciled with

Heaven. He was an aged priest, — the most simple, sincere, and pure-minded of men ; and yet he was a Jesuit. But no one could be more upright and charitable than Abbé Prémord. He was the confessor for a few of the girls, — Abbé de Villèle, the director of the convent, not having time enough to attend to all. We were sent to confession, whether we would or not, once a month, — a detestable custom, which did violence to our consciences and condemned to hypocrisy those who had no courage to resist.

"Father," said I to the Abbé, "you know perfectly well how I have confessed hitherto ; that is to say, that I have not confessed at all. I have only repeated a formula that we have to learn by heart, the same for all who come to confession against their will. You have never given me absolution, and I have never asked for it ; but to-day I do ask you, for I want to confess and repent seriously. I must acknowledge, though, that I do not know what to say ; for I cannot remember any sin that I have deliberately committed. I have lived and thought and believed as I have been taught ; and if I have done wrong not to be a believer, my conscience never has told me so. Nevertheless, I must do penance, undoubtedly; and I want you to direct me, so that I may be able to tell in future what is right and what is wrong."

"Wait a minute, my child," said he; "I see that this is what is called a general confession, and we shall have a great deal to talk about. Sit down."

We were in the sacristy. I took a chair, and asked him if he wanted to ask me questions.

"No," he answered; "I rarely ask any questions, and this is the only one I shall put to you: Are you accustomed to make out your examinations of conscience from the formulas?"

"Yes," I answered; "but there are a great many sins that I cannot tell whether I have committed or not, because I do not understand about them."

"Very well; now I forbid you henceforward to consult a formulary, or to try to learn the secrets of your conscience from any one but yourself. Now let us talk. Tell me simply and quietly all about your life as you remember it, conceive of it, and judge it. Do not arrange anything, or

decide about the right and wrong of the
actions you describe, or your thoughts
either. Do not consider me in the light
of a judge or a confessor, but talk to me
as if I were an old friend. When you have
finished, I will tell you what I should advise
you to correct or encourage in the interest
of your happiness in this world and in the
life to come."

These words, and the kind way in which
they were said, put me entirely at my ease;
and I told him what I could recollect of my
life so much in detail that the story lasted
more than three hours. The good man
listened with fatherly interest and unflag-
ging attention. Several times I saw him
wipe his eyes, especially toward the end,
when I told him simply how I had been con-
verted, just when I least expected it.

The Abbé Prémord was a real Jesuit, but
for all that a conscientious man, with a kind
and tender heart; and his morality was pure,
humane, and human. He never encouraged
mysticism, and exhorted in a practical way,
with a great deal of fervor and kindness.
He told me that I must not lose myself in
dreamy anticipation of a better world, for-
getting how to live well here below; that

is why I call him a real Jesuit, in spite of his sincerity and virtue.

When my story was done, I asked him to condemn what was wrong, so that kneeling before him, recalling those faults in confession and sincerely repenting, I might receive absolution.

"But," he answered, "you have already confessed. If you have not been enlightened sooner by divine grace, it is not your fault. Now, of course, you may be guilty if you neglect to avail yourself of the salutary emotion you have experienced. Kneel to receive absolution, which I will give you with all my heart."

When he had pronounced the sacramental formula he added: "Go in peace. You can take the communion to-morrow. Be calm and joyous; do not torment yourself with useless remorse; thank God for having touched your heart, and let nothing disturb the deep joy of the holy union of your soul with the Saviour."

I communed the next day, the 15th of August, the festival of the Assumption. I was fifteen years old, and had never approached the sacrament since my first communion. It was on the evening of the 4th of August that I had experienced the deep emotion which I called my conversion; so that I had not been long in carrying out the impulse received. I was eager to do something in accordance with my faith, — to testify, as they used to say, before the Lord. This day — really my first communion — seemed the happiest of my life; I was full of overflowing tenderness and assurance of strength. I do not know how I prayed; the consecrated formulas did not suffice. I used them as an act of obedience; but for hours alone in the church I poured out my soul in prayer.

The summer was passed by me in a blissful state of beatitude. I communed every Sunday, and sometimes two days in succession besides. Since then I have shrunk from the materialism of the idea of eating the flesh and drinking the blood of the Divine Being; but then I did not reason, — I was in a bewilderment of joy. I was told: "God is in you, palpitating in your heart, penetrating your life with his divinity; divine grace courses in your veins;" and I accepted as a miracle this complete identification with the Supreme Being. I was consumed like Saint Theresa. I neither ate nor slept as usual; I moved unconsciously; I condemned myself to austerities that were not at all meritorious, — for there was no sacrifice, I felt no exhaustion from fasting. I wore constantly a filigree chain that rubbed my skin like a hair shirt; and when I felt the blood running down my neck, instead of pain the sensation was agreeable. In short, I was in a constant ecstasy; my body had become insensible, and hardly seemed to exist. I was now orderly, obedient, and industrious, as a matter of course, and it cost me no effort. Since my heart was touched, it was not hard to perform my daily duties. The nuns treated me very affectionately,— but I must say that there was no cajolery; they did not seek to stimulate my fervor by any of the means of seduction commonly supposed to be employed in religious communities. Their devotion was calm, a trifle cold perhaps, dignified, even proud. With one notable exception, they had neither the gift nor the desire to proselyte. It may have been characteristic of their order, or else a trait of their nationality.

Madame Alicia was just as kind as ever, — though she did not appear to love me any better after my conversion than she had done before; and this made my affection for her still greater. Enjoying to the full this pure and reliable loving-kindness, I appreciated every day more and more the admirable motherly woman who had cared as much for the rebellious, undisciplined child as for the docile, well-behaved girl I had now become.

Madame Eugénie — who had been so indulgent to me that the girls had accused her of partiality — grew more severe as I became more manageable. Now, when I broke the rules unintentionally or from absent-mindedness, she was often very sharp and exacting; and one day, when I had been so deep in a pious revery that I did not hear what she said, she mercilessly inflicted upon me the once familiar night-cap punishment. A murmur of astonishment rose from the whole schoolroom.

"The idea of making Saint Aurora [a name 'les diables' had given me] wear the night-cap!" "You see how it is," the girls said to one another; "this queer, arbitrary woman really likes 'les diables,' and since Aurora fell into the holy-water font she cannot endure her."

The night-cap, however, did not trouble

me ; for I was sure that I did not mean to do wrong, and I was rather pleased to have Mother Eugénie treat me just as she would have treated another girl in the same circumstances. I did not believe that she loved me any less, for she showed her preference by coming to my cell at night if I had seemed sad or unwell, to ask how I was,— coldly, sometimes ironically, it is true; but to come at all, to show so much interest in me, was a great deal for her to do, and she did it for no one else. I could not open my heart to her as I did to Mother Alicia; but I was not insensible to these marks of affection, and kissed gratefully her cold, long white hand.

XIII.

DURING the height of my first excitement I contracted a friendship considered still more unaccountable than my
partiality for Mother Eugénie, but which
remains one of the dearest and sweetest
memories of my convent life.

One morning as I was crossing the cloisters I saw a lay sister seated on the lowest
step of the staircase leading to the dormi-
tories, —pale, fainting, with beads of perspiration standing on her forehead. On
each side of her was a slop-pail, which
she had brought down to empty; but the
weight and the offensive odor had overcome her courage and strength.

This pale, thin, consumptive-looking woman was Sister Helen, the youngest of the
lay sisters, — the one on whom devolved
the hardest and dirtiest work of the convent. On this account some of the fastidious girls would not go near her, — affecting
to shudder at the idea of her sitting by

them, and carefully avoiding any contact with her garments in passing. She was very plain and ordinary looking, with a cadaverous, freckled face. And yet there was a certain charm about her ugliness; for on looking more closely one saw that her calm, patient expression indicated no stolid indifference, but a long acquaintance with grief and a habit of resignation, and the surmise became a certainty after hearing from her own lips the unvarnished, half unintelligible tale of her humble life. Her teeth were the most beautiful I have ever seen, — white, small, and regular as a string of pearls. When the girls were imagining a perfect beauty, they always gave her Sophia's hair and Sister Helen's teeth.

When I saw her thus fainting, I ran to her assistance, supported her in my arms, and then, not knowing what else to do, said I must go to the work-room for help; but she would not allow that, and reviving a little, tried to rise and take up her pails. But the effort was so piteous that it did not require a great deal of virtue to make me seize them and carry them off. On coming back, I saw her, broom in hand, entering the church.

"Sister Helen," I called out, "you are killing yourself! you are too ill to do any more to-day. Go to bed, and let me tell Poulette to send some one else to do your work."

"No, no!" she answered, shaking her obstinate, bullet-shaped head, "I do not need any help: we can always do what we will, and I choose to die working."

"But that is committing suicide," I said. "God forbids us to seek death, even by toil."

"You don't understand," she interrupted. "I must die soon at any rate, the doctors say; and I had rather go to heaven in two months than linger here six."

I dared not inquire if she spoke thus in hope or in despair; so I merely asked her if she would let me help her clean the church, since it was the hour for recreation, and I should not be neglecting any duties. She consented, saying, "I do not need any help, but we must not hinder charitably disposed persons when they want to do us a kindness." She showed me how to wax the floor of the chancel, and dust and rub with a woollen cloth the nuns' stalls. It was not hard, and I fin-

ished one side of the semicircle while she
did the other; but young and strong as I
was, I became drenched with perspiration,
while she, inured to fatigue, and apparently
quite recovered from her faintness, had
done her part of the work better than
I, though moving sluggishly like a tor-
toise, and looking as if she were ready to
drop.

The next day was a festival; but there
were no holidays for Sister Helen, since the
regular work must be done as usual. I met
her again accidentally as she was going up
to the dormitory to make more than thirty
beds, and she asked me if I would like
to help her, — not, I think, so much perhaps with a desire of being relieved of
her work, as because she began to like
my companionship. I acceded, and should
have done so even before religious fervor
had inspired me with the desire of doing
disagreeable things. When the work was
done (in a time made shorter by my help),
we had a little leisure, and Sister Helen,
sitting down on a chest, said: —

"Since you are so obliging, you might
teach me a little French; it is a great dis-
advantage not to be able to speak the lan-

guage, when I have French servants to direct."

"I am very glad to have you ask me," I responded; "for that shows that you have given up the idea of dying in two months."

"God's will be done!" she said. "I cannot help wishing to die; but I do not pray for death: my suffering must last as long as God wills."

"My good sister, are you then really so very ill?"

"The doctors say so," she answered, "and there are times when I am in so much pain that I think they must be right; but after all, I am so strong that they may be mistaken. However, as God wills." And she rose, saying: "Will you come to my cell to-night? Then you can give me my first lesson."

I consented, making an effort to hide my reluctance. This poor sister was very distasteful to me, — not so much in herself as in her apparel, which was dirty; for her woollen robe had a sickening smell. Then, too, I hated to give up my hour of ecstasy in the church in order to teach French to a person who was not very intelligent, and spoke such bad English.

However, as I had said I would go, that evening I for the first time entered Sister Helen's cell, very agreeably disappointed to find it not only exquisitely clean, but perfumed by the jessamine that grew in the yard under her window. The poor sister was neat also, attired in a new robe of dark blue serge; while the array on her toilet-table showed the care she took of her person. She saw my surprise, and said : —

" You are astonished to find any one so neat and particular who does nothing but dirty work from morning to night. It is just because I am so sensitive to all that is disagreeable and untidy that I have taken upon myself, as a penance, the lowest kind of drudgery. When I first came to France I was shocked to see the dull andirons and rusty fastenings, and did not believe that I could ever be accustomed to live in a country where they were so careless. At home I could see my face in the polished furniture, and all our tins and brasses. But to make things neat you must take hold of what is dirty sometimes ; you see that my taste pointed out the way to salvation."

She said this with the gayety of most valiant persons. I asked her where she

had lived before she came to the convent;
and she began to tell me her story, with
a strong brogue, but in a simple, rustic
idiom whose vigor I am unable to reproduce. This was the substance of her
story : —

"I come from the Highlands of Scot-
land, and am one of a large family of children. My father is a man of strong will.
He is not poor, but he works very hard.
I looked after the sheep, and busied myself within doors taking care of my little
brothers and sisters. We loved each other
dearly. I was happy there in the country, in the fields with the animals; and it
did not seem to me possible to live shut
up, even in a town. I never concerned
myself much about my salvation ; but a
sermon that I heard one day changed all
my ideas, and filled me with such a desire
to please God that I had no longer any
delight or rest at home. The sermon was
about self-renunciation, and when I asked
myself what was the hardest thing I could
do for the love of God, I made up my
mind that it would be to go away and separate myself forever from my family. I
soon became resolved to do so. I went to

the priest whose sermon I had heard, and told him that I had a 'vocation.' He did not believe me, and took me to the bishop, who said: 'Are you unhappy at home? Are you tired of living in the country?' and he wanted to know if anything had happened to make me angry or grieve me. I told him that if that were the case, I should not think my vocation a true one; but I was persuaded that it was not a mere fancy, because leaving home was the greatest renunciation I could possibly imagine. When the bishop had questioned me some time longer, he said: 'Yes, you have a true vocation; but you must obtain your parents' consent.'

"When I went home and told my father, he swore that if I ever went back to see the priest he would certainly kill me. 'I shall go back,' I answered; 'and if you kill me, I shall go to heaven all the sooner. I ask nothing better.'

"My mother and aunts wept bitterly, and reproached me with not loving them, — thus causing me great pain, as you may well think; but I accepted it as part of my martyrdom, and since I could not be cut to pieces or burned alive for the love of God,

I said to myself that I ought to be thankful if my heart is broken in this trial. So I only smiled at the tears of my relatives. I grieved really a great deal more than they did ; but I was rejoiced to suffer.

" I went back to see the priest and the bishop. My father abused me, locked me up in my room, and on the day appointed for me to take the vows he tied me with a rope to the foot of a bedstead ; but I only hoped he would hurt me even more. My mother and aunts, seeing his great anger, and fearing that in a rage he might really kill me, tried to persuade him to let me go. 'Well,' he said at last, 'she may go ; but she will carry away my curse with her.'

" He came and untied me ; but when I fell at his feet and wanted to embrace him, he pushed me away and went out of the house. My poor father was in great affliction ; he had carried his gun with him, and they thought he was going to kill himself ; so my elder brothers followed him, and when I was left alone with the women and children, they all fell on their knees and entreated me to stay with them. But I laughed, and said : ' Beg me as long as you like; you can never make me suffer nearly as much as I hope to.'

" There was one little boy, — the child of my elder sister, — a perfect cherub, whom I had brought up, and who was always hanging about me in the house and in the fields. Knowing how devoted I was to him, they put him in my lap, and he cried and kissed me; but I set him on the floor, took my bundle, and walked to the door. The child got before me, and lying there on the threshold, said: ' If you will go away, you shall walk over me.' I thanked God that he spared me no suffering, and walked over the prostrate, sobbing child.

" As I turned to go away I looked back; and he and all my sisters were crying, holding back the little ones so that they might not run after me. I lifted up my right hand and showed them the sky. My family was not irreligious; they all stopped crying, and there was a great stillness. I walked on, and did not turn around again as long as they could see me. Then I looked once at the roof of the house, and the smoke curling up from the chimney. I was forced to sit down a moment; but I shed no tears, and when I got to the bishop's I was as calm as I am now. He gave me into the care of some pious ladies, who sent me here because they feared that if I stayed near home my father might come and take me away by force."

This simple narrative inspired me with an ardent desire to take the veil, as well as with the most unbounded admiration for Sister Helen. I saw in her a saint like those of old, — rough, ignorant alike of the refinements of life and the subtle casuistry by which we try to reconcile our consciences with our natural affections. She seemed to me a sort of Jeanne d'Arc or Saint Geneviève. She was really a mystic, — the only one in the convent; but then she was not English.

Her narrative produced the effect of an electric shock. I grasped her hands and exclaimed : " You are stronger in your simple might than all the learned men in the world; and I believe that without intending to do so you have pointed out the way I must go; I shall be a nun."

" So much the better," she said, with the artless confidence of a child; " you shall be a lay sister, and we can work together."

It seemed to me that God himself was speaking through this inspired woman. At last I had found such a saint as I had always imagined. The other nuns were earthly angels, who without struggle or suffering enjoyed a foretaste of paradisaic peace. She was more human, and also more divine, — more human because she suffered, and more divine because she loved the suffering. She had not sought happiness and rest in the cloister, — freedom from worldly temptations. Worldly temptations! this poor girl, brought up to hard labor, could not conceive of them, did not know what they were. She had planned and carried out a life-long martyrdom, and had reasoned with the rude, uncompromising logic of the faith of earlier days. Her story made me hot and cold by turns. I saw her in the fields, listening like " la grande pastoure " to mysterious voices in the branches of the trees, and the rustling of the grain. I saw her trampling on the prostrate form of that fair child, whose hot tears fell burning on my heart and then seemed to drop from my own eyes. I saw her alone, standing in the road, cold as a marble statue, and yet with her heart

transfixed by the seven mystic swords, lift-
ing towards heaven her sunburned hand,
and imposing silence by her energetic will
on that sorrowing, unhappy family.

"O Saint Helen!" I said to myself; "you
are right, — you are at peace with yourself. I will be a nun; it will be the despair
of my family, and my own too. But nothing
less than such a despair as that is needed
to give me the right to say to God, ' I love
thee.' I will be a nun, but not an elegant
cloistered lady, living in exquisite simplicity a life of sanctimonious idleness. I
will be a lay sister, doing hard work, — a
servant bowed down with fatigue, cleaning
sepulchres, carrying filth, — anything and
everything, so as to be forgotten after
being cursed by my relatives; so that
with the bitterness of self-immolation for
my meat and drink, God may be the only
witness of my anguish, and his love my
only reward."

11

XIV.

BEFORE long I confided to Mother Alicia my plan of becoming a nun; but she did not seem particularly enchanted with the idea. The excellent, reasonable woman said: "If you like, think it over; but do not take it too seriously. It requires more strength than you imagine to carry out such a project. Your relatives, certainly your grandmother, would never consent. They would accuse us of unduly influencing you, and that is not our way of acting. We never encourage these immature vocations, but prefer to await their development. You do not know yourself yet, and you have a great deal to learn. Come, come, my dear sister! it will be a long day before you sign that;" and she pointed to the formula of her vows in Latin, framed in black over her *prie-dieu*. This formula was irrevocable, binding for life,— not allowed now by French law, but it had been signed in the chancel of the church, on a little table on which stood the Holy Sacrament.

Madame Alicia's doubts annoyed me, and also troubled me a little; but I thought the trouble came from wounded pride, and I persisted in the idea — which I kept, however, to myself — that Sister Helen had a far higher vocation. Mother Alicia was happy; she often said so, simply and without affectation, sometimes adding : " The greatest happiness of all is to be at peace with God. I should never have known that peace in the world, for I am not a heroine; I am conscious of my own weakness, and that makes me timid. I cannot trust myself; the cloister is my refuge, and the monastic rule my moral hygiene. With such powerful aid, I go my way without much effort, or any merit on my part." When, in talking with her, I brought forward some of Sister Helen's arguments, she would gently shake her head and say: " My child, if you seek suffering, you will find plenty without entering a convent. I assure you that a mother, merely in bringing her children into the world, has far more to endure than we ever have. I do not consider the sacrifice we make in taking the veil as anything in comparison with what is daily required of a good wife and mother. Don't worry about it, and wait for the inspiration of God when you are old enough to choose. He is far wiser than we are, and knows what is best for you. If you long to suffer, be sure that life will afford you a great many opportunities; and perhaps if this ardor of self-sacrifice does not die out, you may find that it is not in a convent, but in the world, that you must seek martyrdom."

Her wisdom inspired me with respect, and I owe it to her that I did not make those irrevocable vows which young girls sometimes pronounce in secret before God, — terrible vows, that entail life-long suffering on timorous consciences; vows that may not be broken, mistaken as they are and unacceptable in the sight of God, without a serious shock to the dignity and sanity of the soul.

But I was not proof against Sister Helen's enthusiasm. I saw her every day, and watched for opportunities to help her in her hard work, often giving up my recreation in the daytime for this purpose, and at night teaching her French in her cell.   She

had, as I have said, very little intelligence,
and could hardly write at all. I taught her,
in fact, more English than French, for I
saw that I must begin that way. Our lessons hardly lasted half an hour, for she
became tired very soon, having more will
than intelligence. She never once doubted
my " vocation," and did her best to encourage
me, believing in good faith that I was as
strong as herself. No obstacle embarrassed
her, and she was sure that it would be easy
for me to procure a dispensation enabling
me to enter our convent, in spite of the
rule that excluded all but English, Scotch,
or Irish postulants. I acknowledge that
the thought of being a nun anywhere else
made me shudder, — a proof of the flimsiness
of my vocation; but when I confided these
doubts to Sister Helen, she made light of
them. It has been said that great souls are
never exacting to others, never require from
them such sacrifices as they are willing to
make themselves ; and she who had left her
family and native land, and had entered
unquestioning the first convent proposed to
her, was willing to indulge me in the choice
of a retreat, — thus lessening the sacrifice.
For her it was enough, apparently, that a

girl like me — whom she considered very remarkable because I knew my own language
better than she knew hers — should deliberately propose to become a lay sister instead
of a teacher.

So we built castles in the air together. She
tried to find a good name for me as a sister.
In the community Poulette was called Marie
Augustine, the name I had taken at con-
firmation; so it became necessary to choose
me another. I was to have a cell close
to Sister Helen's, and she authorized me
in advance to devote myself to gardening,
and to cultivate flowers in the yard.

I was very fond of digging, and since I
was too old to have a little garden of my
own, I passed part of my time at recess in
wheeling sods and making paths for the
younger girls. Of course they worshipped
me, but I was well laughed at by the older
pupils. Anna especially sighed over my
infatuation; but she was as affectionate as
ever. Pauline de Pontcarré — one of the
friends of my childhood, who had lately
come to the convent — told her mother one
day before me that I had become idiotic;
that I passed all my time with Sister Helen,
or with " babies " seven years old.

XV.

HOWEVER, one friendship that I had contracted ought to have helped to redeem my character, because it was with the most intelligent girl in the school, — Eliza Austen. Her father, a nephew of the Superior, Madame Canning, had married in Calcutta a beautiful Hindu, by whom he had a great many children, — thirteen or fourteen, I believe. The climate had proved fatal to all but three, — a boy who became a priest; Lavinia, who was with me in the lower class; and Eliza, now Superior in an Ursuline convent in Cork, Ireland.

Mr. and Mrs. Austen seeing their children perish before their eyes, and unable themselves to leave India, confided the three that were left to Mrs. Blount, sister of Mr. Austen and Madame Canning. They were first sent to school in a convent at Cork; but when Mrs. Blount decided to take up her abode in Paris, they all came together. I believe that the father was still away when

I knew the daughters; the mother was living, and had not seen her children for more than twelve years.

Eliza had great beauty and a remarkable mind. Her profile was purely Greek, and her complexion literally like lilies and roses. She had superb chestnut hair, and deep blue eyes that were soft, but penetrating. A singular combination of the two types, — English and East Indian, — she was imperious and fascinating, with the most angelic smile I ever saw. Her low brow, clearly cut features, a certain massiveness in her superbly proportioned figure, indicated a tremendous will, a love of mastery, and inordinate pride. From her earliest childhood inclined to devotion, she came to the convent determined to be a nun, loving but one person, a sister in the Irish convent she had just left, — Maria Borgia de Chantal, who had always encouraged her vocation, and whom she rejoined afterwards when she took the final vows. The greatest proof of friendship that she ever gave me was making me a present of a little reliquary which I still keep on my mantelpiece. I can read even now on the back: " M. de Chantal to E. 1816." She valued it so

highly that she made me promise never
to part with it, and I have kept my word.
It has followed me in all my wanderings.
However, on a journey the glass got broken
and the relic dropped out; but the medallion
remains whole, and the reliquary itself has
become sacred to me. This beautiful Eliza
was the first in all her studies, the best
pianist in the convent, superior to all the
others in everything; because with her
natural talent she had will and patience.
Her object was to be able to teach in the
convent at Cork, which she loved as I did
our own; and Maria Borgia was to her
both Helen and Mother Alicia. More sensible than I was, she was determined to
make herself useful in the monastic life.

Though I now attended to my lessons,
I made hardly any more progress than I did
before my conversion. My only object
being to obey the rules, and my mysticism
impelling me to eschew all worldly vanity,
I did not see why a lay sister that was-to-
be should care to play well on the piano, to
draw, or to learn history. The result was
that at the expiration of three years I was
more ignorant than when I entered the
convent. I had even lost the intermittent

love of study that I had shown as a child.
Devotion absorbed me in a different way, it
is true, but just as completely as the idle
life of my first year. When I had wept pas-
sionately a whole hour in church, I was good
for nothing all the remainder of the day.
The rapture poured out in the sanctuary
unfitted me for secular pursuits, and I had
no enthusiasm, perception, or vigor left, —
no interest in anything. In fact I was becoming stupid, — Pauline was right when
she said so. Yet it seems to me now that I
gained in a certain way; that I was learning to love what was not myself, and that
fanatical devotion has this advantage at all
events, — if it does make you stupid in some
respects, on the other hand it sets you free
from many belittling pre-occupations.

I do not know how it happened that I
became intimate with Eliza. While I was
a "diable" she had been cold and severe
in her manners. She had an overbearing
temper, sometimes hard to restrain, and
when a "diable" disturbed her meditations or meddled with her note-books in
the schoolroom, she turned scarlet with
anger; her beautiful cheeks flushed deeply;
her eyebrows, never far apart, were con-

tracted in a nervous frown; she muttered indignant words, and her ironical smile was terrible, — for her imperious, haughty nature was asserting itself. We used to say that we could see the Asiatic blood mounting to her face. But it was only for a moment; her strong will controlled the angry impulse, — she grew pale, then smiled, and that radiant smile chased away the clouds, lighting up her face like sunshine, and bringing back all its sweetness and dewy beauty. When she revealed herself to me it was not gradually or partially; she candidly confessed her real faults, and confided to me unreservedly the torment of her austere soul. "We are going the same way by different roads," she said one day. "I envy you because your path is so smooth; you do not love the world, and flattery disgusts you. It seems as though you were gliding along from the world to the cloister without effort and without struggle; for you there is no friction. But I," — and as she said this her face shone like that of an archangel, — "I am as proud as Lucifer; I stand up in the temple like a Pharisee, and I have to make a great effort to retreat to the door, where I find you asleep and smiling in the humble place of the publican. I am fastidious even in my choice of a religious life. I am determined to obey, but I feel an ungovernable impulse to command; I am fond of praise, criticism irritates me, and ridicule is exasperating. Naturally, I am neither indulgent nor patient. To conquer all these tendencies, to keep myself from sinning a hundred times a day, I have to make a constant effort; and if I finally succeed in overcoming my evil passions, it will be the result of incessant striving on my part, with a great deal of heavenly help." And then she would weep and beat her breast. I, who felt like a nonentity compared with her, tried to console the weeping girl by reminding her that the greatest saints were those who had had the hardest conflicts.

" That is true," she cried; " there is glory in suffering, and rewards are in proportion to our deserts." Then, covering her lovely face with her beautiful hands, she exclaimed, " And that too is pride! It enters every pore of my body, and takes Protean shapes to conquer me. Why should I long for glory at the end of my struggle, and aspire to a higher place in heaven than yours and Sister Helen's? I am really very unfortunate not to be able to forget myself a single instant."

In such inward struggles and revolts this brilliant girl passed her austerely radiant youth; but it seemed as if Nature had fitted her for the contest, for the more she tormented herself the more superb she was in health and strength, the more wonderful in acquirement.

With me it was different. Without any struggle or storm, I exhausted myself in my devout ecstasies. I began to feel ill, and soon, bodily suffering affecting my state of mind, I entered another phase of this strange life.

XVI.

DURING several happy months the days had sped by like hours. I enjoyed perfect liberty now that I had no wish to abuse my freedom. I spent all my time with the nuns, — in the workroom, where they invited me to tea; in the sacristy, where I helped them fold and put away the decorations of the altar; in the organ-loft, where we practised hymns and choruses; in the novices' room, that served also for music lessons; and finally, in the burial-ground, where the pupils were not usually allowed to go. This cemetery, between the church and the garden-wall of the Scotch convent, looked like nothing but a bed of flowers; for there were no tombs, headstones, or epitaphs, — only the unevenness of the ground showed that there were graves. It was a delightful spot, shaded by fine trees, and adorned with shrubs and bushes as well as flowers. On summer evenings

the air was redolent of the perfume of roses
and jessamine; and even in winter, when
snow had fallen, I have seen tea-roses and
violets blooming on the borders of that
spotless shroud. A pretty rustic chapel —
a sort of open shed, covered with grape-
vines and honeysuckle — sheltered a statue
of the Virgin and separated this sacred
place from the pupils' garden; while our
lofty horse-chestnuts, which overhung the
chapel roof, shaded one corner of the
cemetery. There I have passed hours of
delightful revery. Before my conversion
I used to steal in sometimes to find the
nice india-rubber balls that the Scotch
students had accidentally thrown over the
wall; but now I cared little for india-
rubber balls. I loved to dream of a life
that should be a sort of living death, — of
an existence intellectually torpid, indifferent to all earthly considerations, absorbed
in contemplation without end; and I used
to choose my place in this burial-ground,
and see myself in imagination sleeping in
the only spot in the whole world where I
longed to rest in peace.

Sister Helen encouraged these dreams;
but the poor girl was far from happy her-

self. She still suffered a great deal, although she was better physically, and really seemed convalescent; but I think that much of her suffering was mental, and that she was scolded often, and even persecuted sometimes, for her mysticism. Some evenings I found her weeping in her cell. I hardly dared question her, and indeed it was of no use; for at the first word of inquiry she would shake her head deprecatingly, as if to say: " This is not the first time, — it is nothing you can help." It is true that immediately afterwards she would throw her arms around me, and sob as if her heart would break; but not a word of complaint, not a murmur, escaped from her sealed lips.

One evening when I was in the garden, just under the Superior's window, I heard what seemed to be an angry dispute. I did not catch the words; but I instantly recognized the Superior's voice, harsh and irritated, and Sister Helen's distressed accents, interrupted by sobs. Formerly, in our days of intense excitement about " the victim," I should have stolen up the staircase into the antechamber to find out exactly what was

going on; but now I thought it wrong to
listen to what was not intended for my
ears, and I walked on as fast as I could.
But the heart-rending tones of my dear
Helen kept ringing in my ears. She had
not seemed to be entreating, but protesting
with energy, complaining of some false accusation. Other voices, which I did not
recognize, had chimed in reprovingly or in
accusation; and when I was too far away
to hear anything distinctly, I fancied that
inarticulate cries came to me on the breeze,
mingled with the laughter of the school-
girls in their playground. This was a
deathblow to my serenity. What was
going on in the secrecy of the chapter?
Were these seemingly gentle nuns un-
justly suspicious and cruel to others?

What fault could Sister Helen have committed, saint that she was? Was I concerned
in it in any way? Could they reproach her
with our intimacy? I had distinctly heard
the Superior say angrily, "Shame! shame!"
That she should use such words to a woman
as simple and pure as a little child, — that
she should gratuitously insult an angel,
— offended me bitterly; and a line from
Boileau came irresistibly to my lips: " Can

there be such hate in the soul of the devout?"

It is true that Madame Canning was not quite a female Tartuffe; she had some excellent qualities, but she was harsh and deceitful, as I had reason to know. How could a person in her position indulge in such a torrent of bitter reproach and humiliating threats as the tones of her voice had conveyed to my ears? I asked myself if it were possible for a person of common perception not to love and admire Sister Helen? And then, how could she thus reproach and humiliate any one capable of inspiring so much esteem and affection, — even to do her good, with a view to her ultimate salvation? "Can it be a quarrel, or is it a trial of her patience?" I asked myself. "If it is a quarrel, that is ignoble; and to try her patience thus would be odiously cruel." All at once I heard cries, — possibly the result of my excited imagination; but everything swam before me, and a cold sweat bathed my trembling limbs. "They are beating, they are abusing her!" I cried aloud.

God forgive me for the thought! — it may have been wild and unjust; but I was for the moment possessed by the idea. I was at the farthest end of the garden, but darted like a flash to Sister Helen's cell; and if I had not found her there, I think I should have sought her in the Superior's room. But she had just come in, very much agitated, and her face was wet with tears. My first thought was to look for traces of violence, — to see if her veil was torn, or if her hands were bleeding; for I had suddenly become as suspicious as those are apt to be who pass instantaneously from blind confidence to the agony of doubt. But there was nothing of the kind; only her robe was dusty, as if she had rolled on the floor.

She pushed me away, saying, "It is nothing, — nothing at all. I am very ill, and must go to bed, — leave me!"

I went into the corridor, so that she might go to bed; but I put my ear close to the door. She groaned so that it made my heart ache. As I crouched there, favored by the darkness, there was a constant flitting past me to the Superior's room; doors were continually opened and shut, and rustling robes swept the floor close to me. Then all was still. I went back to

Sister Helen, and said: "I am not going to ask you any questions, for I know that you will not answer me; but let me stay here and take care of you."

She said she was feverish; but her hands were icy, and she trembled all over. She complained of thirst; and since there was nothing but water in her cell, I insisted on going, in spite of all she could say, to find Poulette, whose room was in the same passage. She was in charge of the infirmary, kept the keys, and gave out all the remedies. I told her that Sister Helen was very ill. But to my inexpressible astonishment, good, kind, motherly Poulette only shrugged her shoulders and said, —

"No, she is not very ill; she does not need anything."

Shocked at her inhumanity, I left her at once, and ran to find my friend Sister Theresa, the tall Scotchwoman, the presiding genius of the mint-still in the cellar. She also worked in the kitchen, and I wanted her to heat some water and make a cup of herb tea. But she showed as much indifference as Poulette.

"Oh, Sister Helen!" she said; "she is only in low spirits;" but added presently,

"Well, well! to please you, I will go and get some linden-leaves." And off she went, without hurrying in the least, and with a very contemptuous expression; and handing me at last the herb tea, with a little mint-water, she said: "You had better take some too; it is very good for foolishness and pain in the stomach."

I could get nothing else out of her, and went back to my patient, who had lost all control of herself, and was now in a violent chill. I brought blankets from my own bed, and the hot tea warmed her a little. It was the hour for prayers, and bed-time; so I went to look for the Countess, who refused me nothing now, and asked permission to sit up with Sister Helen, who was very ill.

"What!" she said, looking very much astonished; "she is ill, and there is nobody but you to take care of her?"

"Yes, madame," I answered; "will you give me permission?"

"Certainly, my child; all that you do in that way is right in the sight of God."

And such was my treatment at the hands of this good but ridiculous woman, of whom I had made so much fun, but who never cherished any ill will toward me or any one else, — unless, perchance, they happened to interfere with her parrot Jacquot or Mother Alippe's cat Whisky.

I stayed late with Sister Helen, and only left her when she seemed to be sleeping quietly. For several hours, however, she had suffered tortures, and I heard her ejaculate as she writhed on her bed; "Oh, why can't I die?" But she did not utter a word of complaint or accusation, and the next day she was up and about her work as usual, smiling, almost gay; she had the recuperative power of a child, with the courage and resignation of a saint.

This mysterious occurrence affected me more than it did her to all appearance. I saw from the manner of the nuns and the way I was permitted to see Sister Helen at all hours, that I had nothing to do with the storm that had burst on her head; yet I was shaken not in my faith but in my trustful happiness.

XVII.

ABOUT this time Mother Alippe died
of a prevailing lung fever, with which
the Superior and some of the other nuns
were dangerously ill at the same time. We
had never been very intimate; but I was
always fond of her, and had thoroughly
appreciated, while I was in the lower class,
the uprightness and justice for which she
was remarkable. Her death, after only a
few days' illness, was said to be agonizing,
and the regret for her loss was universal.
Her sister Poulette, who was in charge, as I
have said, of the infirmary, and who also
nursed the Superior and the other nuns,
fainted away at her post, on the day of her
sister's funeral.

There was a poetic sadness about the
beautiful funeral service; the singing, the
tears, the flowers, the prayers at the grave,
the pansies planted immediately on the
place where she was laid to rest (from
which we gathered flowers as mementos),

the resigned grief of the sisterhood, all gave a stamp of sanctity, and conferred a hidden charm on this sudden death, — this separation for a time, as good, courageous Poulette said in talking to us of her sister.

But I had been exceedingly disturbed by something very hard to understand. On leaving our cells that morning we were told that Mother Alippe had died in the night; and though we greeted one another sadly, and some shed tears, there was no violent grief. In fact we had known the night before that she could not recover. Respecting the sleep of childhood, they had not disturbed us when she passed away; we had heard no bell toll, nor anything of the last offices for the dying. We went in to prayers. It was a chilly, foggy morning, and the daylight fell wan on our bowed heads as we knelt in the chapel. All at once, in the middle of the " Hail Mary," a horrible shriek arose from our midst. We all started to our feet terrified, — all but Eliza, who was lying on the floor, writhing in terrible convulsions.

By a strong effort of will she recovered sufficiently to go to mass; but there was a recurrence of the same nervous attack, and she was obliged to leave the church. All day she seemed more dead than alive, and for some time afterwards she would occasionally cry out during her lessons or meditations, and look about her with a startled expression as if pursued by a spectre.

At first these attacks were attributed to violent grief; but then she was not supposed to be more attached to Mother Alippe than many of the other girls. When we were alone she explained it to me. It seemed that only a very thin partition separated her room from the infirmary above, in which Mother Alippe breathed her last. All night long she had heard her dying agony, not losing one word or groan, or the final struggle and death-rattle. It had excited her nervous system so sympathetically that she was obliged to make a tremendous effort not to reproduce it, especially in telling me of this endless night of anguish and terror. I did my best to calm her. There was a prayer to the Virgin that soothed her when she suffered the most, — a little prayer in English, given to her by her dear Madame Borgia, who had told her never to say it alone, carrying out the idea of the primitive Christians, who were fond of repeating:

" Verily I say unto you, where two or three are gathered together in my name, there will I be in the midst of you." For want of a third sympathetic companion, we two used to say it together. Eliza had a *prie-dieu* in her cell, which was furnished like that of a nun. We lighted a pure white taper, and placed before it a bunch of the prettiest flowers we could get; Eliza liked these appurtenances of devotion, and thought they charmed away the mental torture she so often inflicted upon herself. Even Madame Borgia's prayer, however, produced no lasting effect, and the poor girl acknowledged that she had fallen a prey to unreasoning and inexplicable terror. The image of death had presented itself to her in all its grimness. Perhaps her exuberant vitality shrank from the idea of physical annihilation, though she constantly made a free-will offering of herself to God, and in many respects was of the stuff of which martyrs are made. But suffering and death in a material form affected her imagination powerfully. With a brave soul, she had the nerves of a weak woman. She reproached herself bitterly for this weakness, but never succeeded in surmounting it.

I do not know why it should have displeased me so much, but it was another disappointment hard to bear that my noble
Eliza, my ideal of strength and courage,
should be so overcome by anguish at the
solemn death of a sinless human being. I
had no constitutional horror of death myself,
and the philosophical calmness inculcated
by my grandmother was heightened by the
sight of Christian resignation far more impressive than the firmness of a Stoic.

For the first time, death now seemed
dreadful to me from Eliza's unnatural point
of view; and though I blamed her in my
heart for not feeling as I did, I could not
escape the contagion of her terror, and at
night, traversing the corridor near Mother
Alippe's cell, I used to fancy I saw her
ghost flit before me in white robes, which
she shook and waved as she walked. I
could hardly help screaming like Eliza;
and though I had sufficient self-control to
restrain myself, I was deeply ashamed of
this idle terror, which seemed almost blas-
phemous, and became as much provoked
with myself as with Eliza.

XVIII.

BUT I tried in vain to recall my vanishing illusions; gloom settled down on me, and at last one evening in church I found that I could not pray, every effort I made only intensifying my despondency. In fact, I had been really ill for some time, suffering from such insupportable spasms that I could neither eat nor sleep. A girl of fifteen cannot endure with impunity such austerities as those to which I had been subjecting myself, in imitation of Eliza, who was nineteen, and Sister Helen, who was twenty-eight years old.

My strength had evidently given way under my enthusiasm, and for the first time since my conversion I suffered from doubt, — not about religion, however, but about myself. I was persuaded that I had fallen from grace, and repeated to myself over and over again those terrible words, " Many are called, but few are chosen." I began to be sure that God did not love me any more, because I did not love him enough; and I fell into a state of dull despair which I confided to Madame Alicia. She smiled, and tried to explain the connection between my state of mind and physical causes, begging me not to attach such exaggerated importance to these impressions. "Every one has such times of discouragement," she said; "and the more you torment yourself, the worse it will be. Accept this trial in a spirit of humility, and pray that it may come to an end; but if you have not committed any sin of which this dejection is a just punishment, have patience, hope and pray."

What she said was the outcome of her philosophical experience, of her reason and good sense; but my weak head could not accept it. I had enjoyed ardent devotion too much to await its return with patient resignation. Madame Alicia had said, "If you have committed no sin," etc., and I began to think what I could have done; for it was incredible that God should be capricious and cruel enough to withdraw the light of his countenance only to try me. If it were something that came from without, it would be different. " I should gladly accept martyrdom; but if I fall from grace, what can

I do? God is my strength; if he abandons me, is it my fault?" Thus I murmured against the object of my adoration, and like a jealous, irritated lover, I might have become reproachful; but I shrank shuddering from this incipient impiety, and beating my breast, exclaimed: "Yes, it is, it must be, my fault! I must have committed some crime of which my seared conscience has failed to warn me." After a vigorous self-examination, it occurred to me that a series of venial offences might possibly be equivalent to one deadly sin; and I tried to enumerate the sins of omission and commission that undoubtedly I had unconsciously committed,— since it is written that the righteous man sins seven times a day, and that an humble Christian must believe that he sins seventy times seven.

For a long time Abbé Prémord was deceived by my self-deception. In my confessions I accused myself of lukewarmness, of backsliding, of wandering and wicked thoughts, of indifference in devotion, of idleness in school and absent-mindedness at church,— consequently of disobedience; and I said all this without efficacious contrition, or any energy to triumph over temptation.

He scolded me kindly, enjoined perseverance, and sent me off, saying cheerily, "Come, don't allow yourself to be discouraged, and you will yet be victorious."

At last one day when I had gone on accusing myself more vehemently than usual, weeping bitterly all the time, he suddenly interrupted me in the midst of my confession with the abruptness of an honest man tired of wasting his time. "Listen to me," he said. "I do not understand you at all. I am afraid that you are morbid. Are you willing that I should ask the Superior, or any one else you may mention, about your conduct?"

"Of what use can that be?" I answered. "All these kind persons, who are fond of me, will tell you that there is nothing wrong. If I have a hard heart, and have gone astray, no one knows anything about it but myself; and undeserved praise will only make me worse instead of better."

"No, you cannot be a hypocrite," he protested. "Let me make inquiries. I have set my heart on doing so. Come back at four this afternoon and we will have a talk."

I believe that he consulted the Superior and Madame Alicia, and when he saw me

come in he said, smiling: "I knew that
you were demented, and now I am going
to scold you in good earnest. Your conduct is irreproachable; these ladies are delighted with you; you are considered a
model of gentleness, punctuality, and sincere piety. But you are ill, and that af-
fects your imagination. You have become
gloomy, sad, and fanatical. Your companions do not know what to make of you,
and they complain of the change. Take
care! if you go on in this way they will
hate and dread piety, and your example will
help to prevent instead of inducing con-
versions. Your relatives are anxious about
you; your grandmother says that convent
life is killing you, — that you are becoming
a fanatic; and her letters plainly show her
distress. You know that instead of urging
you on, we are all trying to calm you. As
for me, now that I know the truth, I insist
on your giving up this exaggeration. Your
sincerity makes it all the more dangerous.
You must lead a healthy, natural life of
body and mind; and since there is a subtle
pride at the bottom of all these scruples, as
a penance you must take part in the games
and amusements proper for your age. This

very evening you must run about in the garden with the other girls, instead of prostrating yourself in the church for recreation. You must jump rope and play tag. Your appetite and sleep will come back after a while; and when you are in a normal state of health, you will not attach such undue importance to these pretended faults, of which you are proud to accuse yourself."

"Good heavens!" I exclaimed, "that is a harder penance than you imagine. I have lost all taste for games, even the habit of gayety; but I am so frivolous that if I do not keep a constant watch over myself I shall forget all about God and the salvation of my soul."

"Not at all," said he. "Besides, if you go too far, your conscience, when you are well again, will be quick to warn you, and you will heed its reproaches. I tell you that you are ill, and that the feverish aspirations of a delirious soul are not agreeable in the sight of God. What he wants is reasonable service. Go, now, and mind your doctor. In a week I shall expect to hear that you are entirely different in appearance and manners. I want you to be loved and respected, not only by the good girls, but

even more by those who are not good. Let
them see that the path of duty is pleasant,
and that faith is a sanctuary from which
you come forth with a beaming face and
kindly ways. Remember that Jesus told
his disciples to anoint their heads and wash
their hands. He meant, ' Do not imitate
those hypocritical fanatics who put ashes
on their heads, while their hearts are as
unclean as their faces; but be agreeable to
men, so as to make them love the religion
you profess.' My child, you must not bury
your light under the bushel of mistaken
penitence. Adorn your heart with courtesy
and your mind with attractive cheerfulness.
That is natural at your age, and you must
not make people think that piety renders
girls unattractive. God should be loved in
his servants. Come, declare your contrition, say you are sorry, and I will give you
absolution."

"But, Abbé Prémord," I exclaimed, "how
can you want me to amuse myself and
waste all the evening, when I am going to
take the communion to-morrow?"

"Certainly," he answered, "since I tell
you to amuse yourself as a penance, it will
be accomplishing a duty."

"I will do just as you say, Abbé, if you will only promise me that it will be pleasing to God, and that he will give me back the sweet, transporting spiritual ecstasy in which I felt and returned his love."

"I cannot promise that," he said, smiling, "but I should not wonder, — you will see;" and the good man left me stupefied, confounded, frightened, at what he had told me to do.

I obeyed him, however, considering passive obedience a cardinal virtue; and I soon found that at the age of fifteen it is not very hard to get back a taste for jumping rope and playing ball. I joined in these sports after a while without reluctance, then with pleasure, and at last with something of the old zest. Physical activity is so natural for the young! and I had been so long deprived of it that now it had an added charm of novelty. My companions welcomed me back most affectionately; Fanelly first of all, then Pauline, Anna, and the others, — "les diables" as well as the good girls. Seeing me so gay, their first idea was that I was going to be wild again, and Eliza scolded me a little; but I told her and a few others, who sought and deserved my confidence, what Abbé Prémord had said, and they all approved of my conduct.

It happened just as the good confessor had predicted, and I quickly regained moral and physical health.

Six months thus flew by like a happy dream; and I can think of no greater felicity in paradise. Angels seemed to bear me up so that I might not hit my foot against a stone. I did not pray as much as before, because it was forbidden; but when I prayed, all the old ecstasy came back, — though less impetuous, perhaps, than formerly.

XIX.

MY return to gayety made a great change among the older girls. Since my conversion, " les diables " had languished and lost their spirit; but now they revived in the most unexpected way, and became rosewater " diables," — that is to say, gay and frolicsome without disregard of the rules or neglect of their duties. They worked in school-hours, and played in play-time with more alacrity than they had ever shown before. There were no more sharply drawn lines between good girls, stupid girls, and " diables." These last were less obstreperous, the good girls gayer, and the stupid ones acquired readiness and confidence because they were called upon to contribute their share toward the general enjoyment. This great improvement was mainly brought about by a new system of amusement in common. Five or six of the older girls began by getting up charades, — really little plays arranged

beforehand in separate scenes, and acted on
the spur of the moment. Thanks to my
grandmother, I was more conversant with
literature than the others, and I had, moreover, a certain knack in theatricals; so I
came to the front and was made manager.
I chose actors, assigned parts, ordered
dresses, and discovered after a while a great
deal of latent talent among the girls. The
end of the schoolroom toward the garden
was our theatre. The first attempts were
lame enough,—like the historical beginnings
of our national drama; but the Countess
allowed us to go on; then she became interested, and asked Madame Eugénie and
Madame Françoise to come and see for
themselves if there was anything objection-
able in what we were doing, — but these
ladies laughed and approved.

We made rapid progress, borrowed old
screens for side scenes, and accessories
began to shower upon us from all sides.
The girls procured at home materials for
their dresses, but the great trouble was to
get up the costumes for the men's parts.
Not to shock the sisters, we chose the
dress of the time of Louis XIII. Our pet-
ticoats, gathered below the knee, formed

trunk-hose ; and for doublets we slashed the sleeves of our bodices and put them on hind-part before, turning them back at the neck over puckered-up handkerchiefs that represented shirt-fronts. Two aprons sewed together did duty as mantles ; and ribbons, rings, and other gewgaws were not hard to get. When we needed more feathers, we improvised them out of paper cut and curled for the purpose. (School-girls are quick at contrivance, and know how to turn the merest trifles to account.) Then we were allowed to wear boots with spurs, rapiers, and slouched hats, furnished by our parents ; altogether our costumes did very well, and we depended on imagination to supply deficiencies in scenery. After all, it was not very hard to accept a table for a bridge, or a stool covered with green baize for a bank of turf. The younger girls were allowed to be present, and at last we enrolled all who wished to act.

One day the Superior, who was very fond of amusement, sent us word that she had heard a great deal of our theatre, and that she wanted to come with the whole community and see a performance. The Countess and Madame Eugénie had already allowed us to sit up till ten, or even till eleven, when there was a play. For this once the Superior announced that we need not go to bed before midnight, — as much as to say that she expected a fine entertainment. Her request and permission were received with delight. All the girls surrounded me, saying: "Come, author! come, life and soul of the company (this was the last name they had given me), we must go to work. Let us have a superb performance, — six acts, — two or three pieces! Only think! we are to keep our audience on the *qui vive* from eight o'clock till midnight!"

It was a great undertaking to make the Superior and the most serious nuns laugh, and not a slight responsibility either; for the slightest tinge of impropriety might shock the sisters, and put a stop to our theatricals. On the other hand, if the plays proved tiresome, they might close the theatre, giving as a reason that it took too much time, caused too much excitement, and interfered with our lessons, — which was undoubtedly true, especially for the younger pupils.

Fortunately, I was very well versed in

Molière; and leaving out love-passages, I
thought I could arrange enough scenes
for an evening entertainment. Of "Le
Malade Imaginaire" I could make a complete sketch, though I did not remember
perfectly the dialogue and scenic arrange-
ments. Molière's works were prohibited in
the convent; and although I was a manager,
I virtuously refrained from sending for the
books, and merely tried to remember the
story, so as not to be very wide of the mark
in my libretto. I rehearsed some important
scenes, and gave all my actors a general
notion of the main idea of the piece, —
endeavoring to preserve something of the
character of the original. Not one of the
pupils had ever read the play; and since
the nuns did not probably know a line of
Molière, I was sure that it would be a novelty. I have forgotten who took the different parts, but I remember that they were
acted with intelligence and gayety. I was
M. Purgon; and partly because I had forgotten, and partly on purpose, I left out a
great deal of the coarseness.

Every year, on the Superior's birthday,
we had been in the habit of acting pieces,
— not very exciting, I must confess, — gen-

erally taken from the sentimental plays of Madame de Genlis. But the preparations on such occasions were much more elaborate than ours: we had a real theatre, stage properties, footlights, thunder and lightning, parts committed to memory and admirably performed; while now, with my old screens and ends of candles, my actors without previous preparation, a libretto imperfectly remembered, an improvised dialogue, and one partial rehearsal, it was to be feared that I might make a complete failure. But hardly had we begun,— I had only said a few words,— when I saw the Superior unbend, then laugh; while even Madame Eugénie wiped her eyes. It was evidently amusing. Our gayety and animation, the comic genius of Molière,— even so diluted in scraps of recitation and incomplete fragments,— brought down the house. Never in the memory of nuns had they laughed so heartily.

The success of our first scenes encouraged us. I had prepared a sort of ballet interlude, with a comic chase taken from "M. de Pourceaugnac," — only I had charged my actresses to stay behind the scenes (that is to say, the screens), and not to

shoulder their arms until I gave the signal
and set the example. As I saw the audience was so genial, I ventured, and began
the interlude by brandishing the classic
instrument above my head. I was welcomed by bursts of Homeric laughter; for
that sort of thing never seems to shock
devout persons. Immediately my black
regiment in white aprons rushed after me
upon the stage; and this burlesque, for
which Poulette had lent us all the arsenal
of the infirmary, made our audience laugh
so that it seemed as if they might literally
bring down the house. The last thing was
the ceremony of reception; and as I knew
all this part by heart, the girls had learned
some of the verses. The success was complete, and the enthusiasm immense.

From repeating the service constantly,
these ladies knew enough Latin to appreciate the farce of Molière. The Superior
declared that she had never been so diverted
in her life; and I was overwhelmed with
compliments for the wit and gayety of my
inventions. I kept whispering to the girls,
"It is not I, — it is all Molière; I have only
remembered a little." But no one listened
to me, and I was not believed. One of

my friends, who had read Molière, it seemed, in her last vacation, said in my ear : —

"Keep still! What is the use of telling these ladies? Perhaps they would close our theatre if they knew where you got all that. Nothing has shocked them, and there is no harm in keeping the secret, so long as you are not questioned."

In fact, I was credited with Molière's genius. It troubled me a great deal to accept all these compliments, — but I examined myself to see if I felt flattered, and perceived, on the contrary, that one must be crazy to enjoy homage clearly due to another; so I let the mistake pass, and considered it a penance for the sake of amusing my companions. The theatre was not closed, and continued to attract the Superior and the nuns every Sunday.

XX.

IT was not always easy to keep so much exuberant gayety within bounds, and every day it mounted a peg higher. For me, as well as for all the other girls, the air seemed charged with electricity. For instance, though I no longer led the van in ridiculing the poor Countess, and sometimes did my best to prevent the other girls from doing so, — when for the hundredth time, perhaps, she tried to light the candle, cut out of an apple, that Pauline had put in her lantern, or when she used one word for another with the imperturbable absurdity of an absent-minded person, and the whole school shouted with laughter, — I could not refrain from chiming in. Then she would look at me with a distressed expression, and hitching up her great green shawl on her shoulders, ejaculate like Cæsar: —

"And you too, Aurore!"

I wanted to be sorry for what I had done, but she had a way of pronouncing final *e* like *o ;* and when Anna, who was an excellent mimic, turned toward me and said reproachfully, " Auroro! Auroro ! " I could not help it, — my laughter became spasmodic: I should have laughed "through fire and flame," as they say.

Our gayety was so rampant at last that some of the most excitable girls were all ready for open rebellion.   At this time — during the Restoration — there was an epidemic of revolt in convent and board- ing-schools, for girls as well as boys.   When we heard of these occurrences, sometimes serious and sometimes amusing, the live- liest pupils would say : " It is time we had our own little rebellion ; we shall be out of fashion.   Why should we not have a notice in the newspapers, as well as anybody else?" The Countess became nervous, and her severity increased with her alarm.   Some of our good nuns had very long faces, and for three or four days (I believe that our Scotch neighbors had their insurrection at that time) they were evidently in a state of tremulous excitement, which amused us very much.   Then the girls took it into their heads to pretend to revolt, just to see if they could frighten all these ladies, — especially the Countess. They did not take me into their confidence, but hoped that I should be lured on when they had once begun.

One evening in the schoolroom, as we were all seated around a long table, — the Countess at one end busy with her mending, her back turned to a candle, — I heard the girl next me say to her neighbor, " Lift up ! " The word was passed round the table, which, lifted immediately by thirty pairs of little hands, rose higher than the top of the Countess's head. Very absent-minded as usual, she turned, surprised at the sudden disappearance of her light ; but instantly the table and candles fell back to the old level. This trick was repeated several times before she understood what we were about. I was so much amused that I passed on the watchword and " lifted up " with the others. The Countess rose from her seat, trembling with indignation. It had been arranged beforehand that when she did this, each girl should put on a reckless and riotous expression, to frighten her still more. We all folded our arms and scowled like conspirators, and there were murmurs of " Revolt." Quite incapable of asserting herself, sure that the fatal hour had come, she turned and fled like a sea-gull before the storm, — her old green shawl streaming out behind her, — and losing all presence of mind, ran across the garden to take refuge and barricade herself in her own room. As she passed under the windows, we threw out the footstools and candlesticks, without any intention of hitting her; but the flying missiles, and our cries of " Revolt! revolt!" must have seemed to her fiendish.

For a while we were left to our own devices, and we indulged in the wildest merriment; but at last, hearing in the distance the deep voice of the Superior, we knew that the alarm had been given, and that she was coming with some of the older nuns to quell the tumult. Now it was our turn to be frightened; for we had no quarrel with Madame Canning, and since the rebellion was a mere pretence, we did not care to be punished as if we had been in earnest. So we hastily bolted the two doors, recovered the footstools and candlesticks, arranged and relighted our candles; and when order was completely restored, we all knelt down and began reciting the evening prayer, — all but one, who was sent to open the door, at which the Superior had knocked in rather a hesitating way. In the end, the Countess was mercilessly laughed at as a silly visionary; and Maria Josepha, a good-natured servant who attended to the schoolroom, was careful to say nothing of the breakage of some articles of furniture and the demolishing of a few candles. She faithfully kept our secret, and this was the end of the revolution in the convent.

All was quiet, the Carnival was close at hand, and we were getting ready for a finer theatrical representation than we had ever had before. Some play of Molière or Regnard had been chosen for the framework. The costumes were prepared, the parts distributed, and the violinist engaged, — for on that evening we were promised a ball and a supper after the play, with the privilege of sitting up as late as we liked. But a political event, regarded in the convent as a public calamity, put a stop to everything like gayety for the time being.

The news of the assassination of the Duke de Berry was told us by the nuns the morning after the murder, with the most sensational comments. Nothing else was talked of for a week. All the details of the Christian, edifying death of the prince, the despair of his young wife, — who was said to have cut off her beautiful hair to lay it in his tomb, — every circumstance of this royal and domestic tragedy, reported, exaggerated, amplified, and poetized by royalist newspapers and private correspondence, was talked and cried over every day at recess. Almost all the French girls belonged to noble royalist or renegade Bonapartist families. The English pupils — of whom there were a great many — mourned and sympathized on general principles with the Legitimists; and to all of us the story of such a tragic death and the woe of an illustrious family became as exciting as a tragedy by Corneille or Racine. We did not know that the Duke de Berry had been a brutal and dissipated man; he was described to us as a second Henry IV., his wife as a saint, and everything else in accordance.

A whole week of grief is a long time for convent school-girls. One evening some one made a face, another smiled, a third perpetrated a joke, and then we all laughed, rather nervously at first, after so much crying.

XXI.

BUT gradually we resumed our old habits, and the spring wore away. My grandmother had come to Paris, not in a scolding mood after the good reports she had received of my conduct and improvement, and she acknowledged that my simple, natural manners were well suited to a girl of sixteen. She treated me with the greatest kindness; but after a while she seemed troubled. She had been told of my secret wish to become a nun; and a year before, some friends had written to her to say that I looked miserable, and that I was gloomy and fanatical. These reports did not disturb her much, for she said to herself that such a state of mind was too unnatural to last long; but now, when she saw me in excellent health and high spirits, putting on no sanctimonious airs, and yet unaffectedly eager to get back to the convent as soon as possible, she became alarmed, and determined that I should return with her to Nohant.

This announcement fell like a thunder-bolt out of a clear sky into my happy life, — the most perfect happiness I have ever known. The convent was for me an earthly paradise. I was neither a pupil nor a nun, but something between the two, with abso-lute freedom in a place which I never left, even for a day, without deep regret. No one could have been happier. I was sur-rounded by friends, a recognized leader in all pleasures, and the idol of the little girls. The sisters, seeing me so cheerfully per-sistent in my vocation, began to believe in it themselves, and forbore all opposition. Eliza, the only one who had understood my recent gayety, was convinced that I was thoroughly in earnest, and Sister Helen abated no jot of her enthusiasm. I was sure myself of not being mistaken, and re-mained so long after leaving the convent.

Madame Alicia and Abbé Prémord were the only persons who still doubted, — prob-ably because they knew me better than any one else. "Entertain this idea, if it makes you happy," each said separately, in almost the same words, "but make no im-prudent vows or secret promises to God ; above all, do not lisp a word to your relatives of your determination till you are perfectly certain that it is irrevocable, — till you know positively that it is a permanent and not a transient longing. Your grandmother has set her heart on your marriage. If that does not take place, however, in two or three years, and you still feel as you do now, we can then talk it all over."

The good Abbé had made it very easy for me to be amiable. At first I had been alarmed at the idea that it would be my bounden duty to use any influence I had with my companions to try and convert them.

" I hope you will do nothing of the kind," he said one day when I told him what I dreaded. " Never be a bore ; preaching to your companions would be in very bad taste at your age. Be pious and cheerful ; that is all I ask of you. Your example will preach better than any injunctions."

My excellent old friend was right to a certain extent. It is true that my influence was not bad ; but religion so gayly inculcated had made the girls very lively, and I am not at all sure that it is an infallible recipe for turning out good Catholics. I myself, however, remained a fervent be-

liever, and should always have been so, I
think, if I had stayed in the convent; but I
was obliged to go away, and forced, moreover, to hide my grief from my grandmother, who would have been deeply distressed if she had known what pain it
caused me to part from all these beloved
objects. It nearly broke my heart. But
when the dreaded moment came, I did not
shed a single tear. I had had a month
to prepare for the separation, and I was
so resolved to submit without a murmur,
that to my grandmother I seemed calm
and contented. But my wretchedness was
great, not only then, but for a long time
afterwards.

XXII.

I MUST not close this account of my convent life without recording that I left behind me grief and consternation on account of the death of Madame Canning. Since my conversion I had felt it my duty to show her proper respect, but she never attracted me ; yet I was told that I was one of the last persons she mentioned affectionately before she died.

This powerfully organized woman was admirably fitted, in many respects, for the position she held in the convent, over which she had reigned supreme since the time of the Revolution. She left the community in a very prosperous condition, with a large number of pupils, and with social relations that seemed to insure the most desirable kind of patronage. However, from the day of her death there was a decline of prosperity. Madame Eugénie was immediately chosen as her successor, and if I had remained in the convent I should have been

more indulged than ever; but she had no
administrative ability like Madame Canning's. I do not know whether it was her
fault, or that of her coadjutors; but after
a few years she asked permission to retire,
and it was gladly granted, — for she had
either mismanaged, or had been unable to
prevent mismanagement.

There is a fashion in everything in this
world, — even in convent schools. Ours
had been in vogue under the Empire and
during the Restoration. The greatest families in France were represented there, —
the Mortimers and Montmorencies, for instance, sending their daughters as pupils.
Later, the children of those imperial gen-
erals who had made their peace at the
Restoration were admitted, — their parents
hoping, doubtless, that they might form
aristocratic friendships and alliances. Now,
however, had come the turn of " la bour-
geoisie; " and although I heard afterwards
some of my grandmother's old friends accuse Madame Eugénie of vulgarizing her
convent, I remember perfectly that when
I left, shortly after the Superior's death,
" le tiers état " was already represented, —
greatly to the pecuniary advantage of

the community. In fact, this move was considered at the time the crowning glory of Madame Canning's prosperous rule.

I had seen our ranks rapidly filled up with a number of charming girls, daughters of merchants and manufacturers, — quite as well-bred as the scions of noble houses; and it was a generally recognized fact that some of them were more intelligent than their aristocratic companions.

It proved to be, however, a short-lived prosperity; the heads of noble families thought that the convent was becoming plebeian, and took away their children. The fashion veered, and the prestige of great names now belonged to the " Sacré Cœur " and the " Abbaye-aux-Bois." Several of my companions were transferred to those convents; and little by little the aristocratic element was eliminated, — the old retreat of the Stuarts deserted by the Legitimists. Then, of course, the bourgeois, who had flattered themselves that their children might become intimate with the daughters of the nobility, were chagrined and disappointed; or perhaps the Voltairean spirit of the reign of Louis Philippe, which had been smouldering ever since the beginning of his predecessor's rule, rendered convent education more unpopular.

However that may be, after a few years I found our convent depopulated, — seven or eight little girls only, instead of seventy or eighty pupils; and the empty house seemed given over to silence, instead of the constant stir and occasional tumult of old times.

Poulette was still at her post, complaining loudly of the new Superior, and bemoaning the downfall of their ancient grandeur.

Later, — I think in 1847, — some one told me that there were more pupils; but after this decadence the convent never recovered its former prestige.

The change can be accounted for only by supposing that it was one of Fashion's unjust caprices; for after all, these English nuns were "wise virgins," and in the course of a quarter of a century they could scarcely have lost all that charm which belonged to their kind, gentle, reasonable ways.

THE END.